# PRAISE FOR
# SEO *for* GROWTH

"*John and Phil hit the nail on the head. The way people shop and buy has fundamentally changed, an inbound strategy is now a necessity for getting found online and growing your business.*"
**Brian Halligan,** Co-founder and CEO, HubSpot

"*Too many web designers and business owners treat SEO as an afterthought. SEO For Growth will show you how to build a lead generating website from the ground up.*"
**Larry Kim**, Founder and CTO, WordStream, Inc.

"*SEO for Growth is stunning in its practicality and relevance. Every reader will make money, save money, or both thanks to this guide.*"
**Jay Baer**, President of Convince & Convert and Author of Youtility

"*Business owners really need to read SEO For Growth. This book will take the mystery out of SEO and Google rankings in one weekend.*"
**Michael Port**, NY Times Bestselling Author of Book Yourself Solid

"*There are many pieces to solving the SEO puzzle. From search engine friendly web design and content marketing, to social media and reputation management, SEO for Growth will help you put it all together.*"
**Joost de Valk**, Founder and CEO, Yoast

*"This is a must-read Internet marketing book for entrepreneurs and executives alike. Read it. Now. Do it. Live it. Then watch your business grow."*
**Dave Kerpen**, CEO, Likeable Local and NY Times Bestselling Author of The Art of People

*"If you're looking to learn about SEO, this book gives you a great way to get started."*
**Eric Enge**, CEO, Stone Temple Consulting and Co-author of The Art of SEO

*"Customers are looking, but can you be found? SEO for Growth provides a complete SEO roadmap to all the right places from content to keywords to analytics so your customers can easily find your business and your business can find success."*
**Lee Odden**, CEO, TopRank Marketing

*"If you lack a geek gene but need to figure out how to make SEO work for you and your business, this is the book you need. It's practical, actionable, clear, and flat-out useful. But more than that.. it's also stupid-simple (and I mean that in the best possible way)."*
**Ann Handley**, Chief Content Officer, Marketing Profs, Author of Everybody Writes and Content Rules

*"To say I wouldn't normally pick up a book called SEO for Growth is an understatement. I was very pleasantly surprised by how applicable and useful this book is. I even stole several great ideas for my own sales efforts."*
**Chris Brogan**, CEO, Owner Media Group, Inc.

*"At the beginning of Chapter 1 of SEO for Growth, Phil and John share a quote from me about how effective SEO can't be divorced from marketing. It is first and foremost a marketing discipline. I couldn't be more pleased to have that quote appear in this book, because SEO for Growth lives and breathes that principle. You'll find it to be an excellent guide to not just 'doing SEO,' but creating search marketing that builds your business."*
**Mark Traphagen**, Senior Director of Marketing, Stone Temple Consulting

# SEO *for* GROWTH

## The Ultimate Guide for Marketers, Web Designers & Entrepreneurs

JOHN JANTSCH
—— *and* ——
PHIL SINGLETON

*"If you want a comprehensive guide to SEO this year, look no further. This actionable guide walks you through the basics of SEO all the way to advanced strategies and techniques. This is my new go-to guide for anyone looking to quickly learn the ins-and-outs of SEO."*
**Brian Dean**, Founder & CEO, Backlinko

*"Networking and referral marketing will always be critical small business marketing tactics, but today's buyer often follows a word-of-mouth recommendation with a Google search. SEO for Growth will show you how to create a web presence that will help you convert more of your referral leads."*
**Dr. Ivan Misner**, Founder of BNI and NY Times Bestselling Co-author of Masters of Networking

*"A business website should be a marketing platform, not just a digital brochure. Read SEO for Growth, a light-bulb will go off. You'll never look at your website the same way again."*
**Clate Mask**, Co-founder & CEO, InfusionSoft

*"I have seen way too many businesses busy playing catch-up with their SEO. They would rather cut corners and then fix their mistakes (which may have long-lasting effects) rather than being more proactive about their search marketing. John and Phil's SEO For Growth can help businesses and entrepreneurs adopt a growth mindset instead of continuously putting out fires. I recommend SEO For Growth to anyone who needs a no-nonsense, cutting-edge approach to their search marketing efforts.*
**Kelsey Jones**, Executive Editor of Search Engine Journal and CEO of StoryShout

*"Great to see that John and Phil have written a powerful resource that creates the focus on SEO that it needs. Ignore this book at your peril. I didn't focus enough on search when I started out but then discovered it's importance, and today over 50% of my traffic now comes from SEO. It drives 300% more traffic than social! "*
**Jeff Bullas**, CEO, JeffBullas.com

*"If you are just getting started in SEO, or wanting a quick primer to understand how Google views and ranks websites, SEO for Growth is a great resource. It highlights the most important things for a business owner to know to ensure they are setting their website up for success in the eyes of Google."*

**Jennifer Slegg**, Founder and Editor, The SEM Post

*"SEO isn't dead. In fact, until the internet comes to a close, you can be assured that 'getting found' online will impact every business, every brand, and everyone's bottom line. And that's exactly why SEO for Growth is so very important."*

**Marcus Sheridan**, President, The Sales Lion

*"SEO for Growth is a fantastic resource for marketers from all walks of life. I couldn't think of two better people than Phil and John to take a relatively difficult topic and break it down into something so easily digestible. This book is also one of the most practical and actionable SEO resources I've seen and will be an important one to refer to many times over."*

**Dan Olson**, CEO, UpCity

*"Unlike the previous generation of SEO guides, this book doesn't teach marketers how to game the system for a short-term win. It coaches you on how to play the game—and be successful—your entire career."*

**Jon Hall**, CEO of Grade.us

*"Once upon a time a Search Engine Optimizer (SEO) would walk into a bar, pub, club, and have a drink, of beer, lager, wine, white wine, French wine, champagne...*

*But as someone who has built authority through Social SEO, successfully creating communities around content, I can assure you times have changed. Now, if you want Google to serve you well, then it is time to see the virtual bar has been refurbished.*

Listen closely to John and Phil, and follow the experts throughout this book, to be first in line and stand head and shoulders above the rest of the crowd."

**Martin Shervington**, Official Google Small Business Advisor, PlusYourBusiness.com

"If you feel lost when it comes to SEO, read SEO for Growth and you'll know more about digital marketing than most so-called SEO experts out there."

**Josh Steimle**, MWI

"There's no need to be intimidated by online marketing. SEO for Growth is the perfect guide to help you learn how to use the Internet to successfully grow your business."

**Mike McDerment**, Co-Founder & CEO, FreshBooks

"SEO for Growth provides a clear roadmap to ensure SEO is a key channel for any company's customer acquisition strategy. A must-read for anyone looking to grow their business."

**John Clark**, Founder & CEO, Rival IQ

"I knew this book was a winner the minute I read the table of contents and saw a section entitled 'A Website is not a Marketing Plan.' In my experience with clients in the B2B space there is a lack of understanding of how search engines work, or how to create online experiences with both prospective customers and search engines in mind. This practical guide walks you through every step of the equation: how to optimize for search, how to use knowledge of search and apply it to your customers' buying journeys, how to write compelling content for each stage of the customer journey, the power of online reviews, and much, much more. With this book in hand, marketers will be better equipped to deliver real value."

**Shelly Kramer**, CEO, V3 Broadsuite

*"A fast and secure website is surely critical for your online business success, but rarely enough if you don't have a solid marketing and growth strategy in place. SEO for Growth is the most comprehensive guide to the ever-changing marketing realm that every business owner needs to read at least once!"*
**Tenko Nikolov**, CEO, SiteGround Web Hosting

*"SEO for Growth should be bought by every Marketer, Web Designer and Entrepreneur. It sheds much needed light on the dark art of SEO by delivering practical knowledge on how to integrate SEO across the entire digital customer journey. I wish I had this book five years ago when I started Nimble.com. John and Phil have a winner with this book!"*
**Jon Ferrara**, Founder & CEO, Nimble.com

*"Practical, plain-English SEO advice that you can learn in SEO for Growth, or learn the hard way. John and Phil cut through two types of piffle: what desperate marketing 'experts' tell business owners, and what too many frustrated business owners tell themselves. The advice in Chapter 5 alone will save you an ulcer or two. "*
**Phil Rozek**, Owner, Local Visibility System, LLC

*"Your website should work as hard for your business as you do. SEO For Growth is an excellent SEO guide to help you make sure that it does."*
**Jeniece Primus**, Co-founder, Emphatic.co

*"If there's one thing I've learned as a content marketer and business owner, it's that you have to stay up on your knowledge of Google and its ever-changing world of algorithms. The down-to-earth, practical, solid advice laid out by two top experts (John & Phil) in SEO for Growth make it a wonderful book for any serious web marketers who need to know SEM from the ground up, as well as stay up on it (the recommended expert sections help you know just who to follow and why). Every website owner needs to have this on their desk."*
**Julia McCoy**, CEO of Express Writers, Author of So You Think You Can Write?

*"Don't limit your business by delaying your SEO efforts. Time is critical with SEO and SEO for Growth does a fantastic job of explaining how to put it all together as you grow your business."*
**Jason VandeBoom**, Founder & CEO, ActiveCampaign

*"Copyblogger's Brian Clark, who wrote the foreword for this book, states it the best: 'if you want to grow your business, you can't avoid Google.' This book, SEO for Growth, is the playbook your business needs to win with Google and see the growth you deserve. I absolutely loved the 'Quick Tips' shared throughout this must-read book and know you will also."*
**Mike Kawula**, CEO, Social Quant

*"Once I started reading this book I could not put it down, and I've been in the SEO industry since 1998. I really enjoyed the section on Google algorithms, especially Panda & Penguin along with the Importance of SSL."*
**William Rock**, Marketing Strategist / Coach, William Rock LLC www.williamrock.com

*"These days, there is far too much reliance on spending on paid search, display & other advertising to drive quality leads & sales. John & Phil lay out a practical & actionable approach to creating a successful SEO strategy that is relevant to novices and experienced marketers alike."*
**John Hingley**, Co-founder, Dasheroo

*"SEO can be a powerful channel to reach new customers — or a source of endless frustration. SEO for Growth will help turn SEO into a competitive advantage for your business."*
**Andy Powell**, Co-founder and CEO, CallRail

*"SEO for Growth gives you everything you need to reliably generate high quality traffic. It does a great job covering one of the most effective (and accessible) ways of marketing a business."*
**Ruben Gamez**, Founder, Bidsketch

"*John Jantsch has been a digital marketing champion and leader for SMBs longer than almost anyone. His advice will help you find the ROI in your marketing efforts. I first read his Duct Tape Marketing program over a decade ago, and everything that I've read from John is spot-on. This book is no different. Read it. Apply it. And your business will grow.* "

**Travis Wright** @teedubya, Chief Marketing Technologist, CCP.Digital

"*SEO is one of the most snake-oil infested areas of marketing today. Many business owners pay handsome fees to agencies who simply outsource it to low-cost foreigners who do... 'who knows what'. They take credit when things work and find someone to blame when they don't. Armed with this guide you'll know what to do if you're doing SEO yourself; and you'll know exactly what your experts should be up to if you hire them. Phil and John's priority list of target review sites for small businesses alone is worth the price of admission.*"

**Perry Marshall**, Author
Ultimate Guide to Google AdWords
Ultimate Guide to Facebook Advertising
Ultimate Guide to Local Business Marketing
80/20 Sales & Marketing

"To every hardworking, big-dreaming entrepreneur out there making the world a better place for us all."

JOHN JANTSCH


"To my twin sons Ely and Ostyn. Don't ever worry about what other people think about you, and always remember that you can do anything you put your mind to."

PHIL SINGLETON

# CONTENTS

# FOREWORD
## By *Brian Clark*

Since you've opened this book, I'm guessing you want to grow your business or generate more leads for your clients.

So, congratulations! A commitment to life-long learning is the hallmark of any truly devoted entrepreneur.

As a marketer and an entrepreneur myself, I've been where you probably are *right now*. I've founded and invested in some pretty big wins. And, like most entrepreneurs, I've had my share of failures. I know how important growth is to your business and how challenging lead generation can be.

I've spent a lot of time in, and around, the SEO industry. I've presented and written extensively on search engine optimization and content marketing. One thing is for certain: if you want to grow your business, you can't avoid Google.

What I love about *SEO for Growth* is how it explains SEO and Internet visibility in the broader context of marketing and brand building. In other words, SEO isn't the icing or the cake, it's the sugar that's baked in from the start. As is the case with any winning recipe, if you don't get the ingredients right, the dish will either fail or never reach its full potential. Yet, many businesses treat SEO as an afterthought.

Before you dive into the first chapter, here are few thoughts to keep in mind.

First, this book provides a really interesting perspective. On one hand, you have John Jantsch, a man who is synonymous with small business marketing expertise. Co-author Phil Singleton, on the other hand, is an accomplished digital agency owner with a ton of Main Street experience. The balance of this coach-and-player relationship really shines through as John and Phil lead you from strategy and planning through web design and content marketing, explaining how to weave in SEO best-practices along the way.

Second, *SEO for Growth* is a perfect example of the strategy and tactics it espouses. Visit the SEOforGrowth.com website, and you will see how John and Phil practice what they preach. From blogging and guest blogging to podcasts and eBooks, this book is a living example of content-driven SEO. You have as much to learn from the way the book was marketed and promoted as you do from its content.

*SEO for Growth* has exactly what you need to build and power a lead-generating website. But don't just take my word for it. Take a close look at the testimonials and reviews. *SEO for Growth* has been recommended by some of the biggest names in business, from tech company CEOs and marketing influencers to *New York Times* best-selling authors and nationally recognized SEO experts.

Finally, reading a great book on SEO will only get you so far. Many business owners will be motivated by the advice in its pages, but in reality, very few will act on it. This is an enormous opportunity for you. If you simply apply what you learn from this book and commit to SEO for the long haul, you will generate more business and more leads, period.

Yours Truly,

*Brian Clark*
Founder & CEO, Rainmaker Digital

*Introduction*

# THE NEW RULES
# OF SEO

In 2001, Danny Sullivan used the term "Search Engine Marketing" to describe an ever-growing list of practices related to being found on the Internet. **Search engine optimization**, or SEO, specifically relates to how websites and other online content is found and listed among a search engine's unpaid or "organic" results. Today, the industry has a vast array of professionals working to improve SEO so companies can reap its rewards. It has become one of the fastest-paced industries in history and has had an impact on nearly every business sector.

Each year, some of the smartest people in the world work with some of the most powerful and influential companies to build intelligence in the SEO sector. SEO is always changing; falling behind can result in a crushing blow for many businesses.

Over the last decade we've witnessed a systematic dethroning of old marketing and advertising techniques and a complete overhaul of what it means to be a 21st-century marketing machine. The new rules of marketing decide which businesses succeed and which fade away. Without adequate knowledge of current search engine marketing trends, entire marketing teams flounder in the dark. The companies rising to prominence today are those that take the importance of SEO, and the new marketing practices it requires, seriously. Moving forward, SEO will be one of the first lines of defense against competitors and the most direct way to reach your ideal customers.

SEO has come a long way since the days of "hoodwinking" search engine *algorithms*. The industry is constantly evolving and has recently experienced a major shift. It began in 2013, and we are now well beyond the tipping point. There are a whole new set of rules governing SEO in the modern marketing context. SEO is now inextricably linked to *content marketing* and other new methods of Internet marketing.

As the Google search engine *algorithm* continues to evolve, your practices need to change with it. These are trends and practices that you need to embrace now, before the transition leaves your business stuck in the sinking sand of inaction or at risk from employing dated SEO tactics.

This book is for website designers and marketers, as well as business owners and entrepreneurs, who want to understand and apply SEO best practices. We have created this book to explain — in the simplest manner — what you need to do to get and maintain results in the new era of content-driven SEO.

The authors, John Jantsch and Phil Singleton, have helped thousands of businesses leverage the Internet to increase revenues and profitability. By combining John's powerful Duct Tape Marketing System with Phil's years of SEO experience at the local, regional, and national levels, the authors have created a systematic approach to SEO that is highly effective, sustainable, and easy to understand.

*Let's get this SEO party started.*

# DEFINING SEO
# FOR GROWTH

*"SEO just can't be effective for long-term business growth these days unless it is integrated into a holistic marketing approach. Today more than ever, SEO is a part of marketing and can't be divorced from it."*

Mark Traphagen, Stone Temple Consulting

**Search Engine Optimization** is one of the most confusing marketing terms of the modern marketing era.

It's not that people don't understand SEO — okay, maybe it kind of is — it's that the very nature of SEO seems to shift with each new pronouncement from Google.

One thing is eternally clear, however. Showing up — preferably towards the top of page one — when someone goes looking for an answer, product, or solution, is a determining factor in the success and growth of just about every business.

Today, marketers must understand that the most significant objective in marketing is to be discovered.

CEB recently conducted a survey of over 2,200 B2B buyers, and it found that *57% of the purchase decision is complete before a customer even calls a supplier.* [1]

Take a few minutes to visit the following website link and read through the glossary of terms:

**https://seoforgrowth.com/seo-glossary**

Words and phrases in both ***bold and italics*** are defined on the above web page. Familiarizing yourself ahead of time with some commonly used SEO terms will make this book a smooth read.

## It's All About Self-Discovery

Buyers no longer value mass-produced information fed to them through automated marketing funnels designed to create product demand. There is no straight path to any purchase today. Buyers wind their way through a series of experiences and eventually fulfill some purpose by making a purchase. Google actually refers to this as the Path to Purpose,[2] and it sums up the new buyer behavior perfectly.

The top sites on the Internet are all sites that allow the user to find things: Google, Facebook, YouTube, Baidu, and Wikipedia. Today's consumer has grown addicted to instant information and places higher value on information they've discovered on their own through sites they

---

1    B2B Digital Evolution. Think With Google. https://www.thinkwithgoogle.com/articles/b2b-digital-evolution.html

2    When the Path to Purchase Becomes the Path to Purpose. Think With Google. https://www.thinkwithgoogle.com/articles/the-path-to-purpose.html

have grown to trust, such as Google. Increasingly, if you're not found in search, you don't exist. You may be better equipped to solve your customers' needs, but you won't get the opportunity to show them that if they don't discover you in their buying hunt.

## SEO as Channel

Given this vast change in buyer behavior, SEO has risen from the ranks of technical tactic to a full-blown marketing and growth channel.

Today, SEO must be considered in parallel with other established lead channels such as Public Relations, Advertising, and Referral Generation. But it's not enough to simply add SEO practices to the mix; you must also consider when, where, and how SEO can make the greatest impact.

It most certainly is not a one-size-fits-all bag of tricks. This book will show you, in tremendous detail, how to employ the right tactic at the right time.

## The Context of SEO

*SEO for Growth* is as much about strategy and mindset as it is about technical know-how. It's also about discipline, patience, and consistency. You can't achieve the greatest possible results without laying a firm foundation and integrating SEO practices with social media and content. It's all connected.

To get the most from any *SEO for Growth* practice, it's essential that you understand the context in which SEO can most effectively be employed.

There are three stages of growth through which every business must pass: traction, expansion, and **conversion**. You must align the proper marketing tactics with each of these stages, and this most certainly includes SEO tactics.

As you dive deeper into subsequent chapters, keep your business's current growth stage in mind and try to determine how you can best apply specific tactics.

## Traction SEO

In the traction stage, you're still trying to find that perfect match between ideal customer and market message. Your product or service is evolving, and it's a pretty good bet that you don't have sufficient content or *domain authority* to get your content to rank, no matter how much optimization you perform.

That's your job at this stage — to create content and make sure that your website is fully optimized. Plan your editorial calendar and go to work on creating, at a minimum, one piece of epic content per week. Content is the heart of modern SEO. Without valuable content, your SEO efforts can't take root. We know that a term like "epic content" is both vague and scary, but know this — the days of thinly written, 500-word "SEO blog posts" are over.

SerpIQ's 2012 study of over 20,000 keywords showed that the top-ten results of each had an average content length of more than 2,000 words. The average number of words for the content in the number-one spot was 2,416. For the #10 spot, the average number of words was 2,032. To this day, well-written, authoritative, long-form blog posts significantly outperform filler blog posts.

The good news is that if you create truly useful content (blog posts, videos, *SlideShare* presentations, *podcasts*, etc.), you can use it in your *lead capture pages* and *conversion* efforts even as you begin to impact *organic traffic* numbers.

## Expansion SEO

In the expansion stage, you've found some things that work. Your *value proposition* is getting easier to explain, and your content efforts are starting to pay dividends.

Expansion is all about sustainability and increased growth rate. It's about retaining customers and finding ways to leverage relationships to do more.

The primary tool for expansion SEO is *content marketing* and the natural *link building* that comes with it. Here again we've used another one of those scary SEO terms. Link building in the traditional old-school SEO way of thinking was all about getting other websites to link back to yours as a way to show good old Google that lots of people liked your content. Today, link building has a lot more in common with networking. The quality of your *backlinks* is more important than the quantity. Once again, content plays the major role. One of the best ways to acquire high-quality, relevant backlinks is to take your epic content and start offering it to others.

Although the need for content marketing and link building applies even to someone just getting started, we think you reap the most benefits from these efforts when you already have some of your best content on your site.

## Conversion SEO

The conversion stage is, of course, where the money is. During this stage, you want to start leveraging the assets you are building.

By this time, you have weaved SEO into the DNA of your company, and your website has become the hub for all your marketing efforts.

During this stage, terms like "domain authority" will start to get very interesting.

*Domain Authority* is a scoring system devised by SEO software company Moz to estimate how a website will rank in search engine results. Points are awarded for each factor Moz believes search engines use to rank any domain (i.e., your URL or website address), and the cumulative score, out of 100, is a site's Domain Authority. There are numerous elements that go into constructing this score, but suffice it to say that working to achieve a higher Domain Authority is a much healthier and sustainable approach to SEO than working to acquire as many backlinks as possible. You can find a more detailed description of Domain Authority from Moz here:

https://moz.com/learn/seo/domain-authority

The reason we call this the conversion phase of SEO is that once you start receiving traffic, you go to work on making that traffic pay — that is the point of all this, after all. One highly ranked, shared, and linked-to blog post can turn into a lead-generation gold mine with a few simple conversion tactics.

For example, take the time to learn about building Facebook audiences, and you'll discover that you can effectively "*pixel*" visitors to your one or two winning posts so that you can continue to market to them on Facebook or even build what Facebook calls "lookalike" audiences. That's how you cast an even wider net to drive traffic to your site.

Of course, once you start getting traffic to certain posts — even if only one or two — you have the foundation on which to build content upgrades that allow you to capture highly targeted leads by offering a video or checklist to accompany the post in exchange for the reader's email address.

With the right content, we've seen conversion rates as high as 40%, meaning 40% of the people visiting a page took the offer for the upgrade and provided their email address.

Since you've read this far, you might be thinking that we're not even talking about SEO at this point — **and that is precisely the point**. You can't have an effective SEO approach without understanding how to integrate your SEO channel into with your overall marketing and growth plan.

In the chapters that follow, you will be introduced to the finer points of SEO practice, not simply to show you the tools of the SEO trade, but to equip you — the marketer, web designer, or entrepreneur — with the knowledge and mindset to understand the role of search engine optimization in every aspect of your and your clients' growing businesses.

We have two goals that we want you to achieve by reading this book. First, we want you to understand exactly how modern SEO can improve your business in the new search engine economy.

Second, we want to share some of our strategies and tactics to get you started. Now, let's get you up to speed on search engines.

## Expert to Watch: *Michael Port*[3]

Why should you pay careful attention to Michael Port? Only because he is one of the most well-rounded and successful entrepreneurs in the industry.

Of his six books on business development and communications, two of them, *Book Yourself Solid* and *Steal the Show*, made it to the best sellers lists of the New York Times, the Wall Street Journal, USA Today, and Publisher's Weekly. Amazon and 800-CEO-READ also included both books in their lists of the best books of the year.

While not the first person many associate with SEO, Michael is an expert marketer and authority on public speaking. In fact, he's one of the best speakers working today. His two companies, Book Yourself Solid Worldwide and Heroic Public Speaking, teach marketing and public speaking, respectively, to entrepreneurs and executives alike.

Michael appears frequently as a business-development and communications expert on MSNBC, CNBC, and PBS. He is also the host of the most popular podcast on the topic of public speaking and performing, Steal the Show with Michael Port. Follow Michael on Twitter @michaelport.

---

3   http://www.michaelport.com

# THE SEARCH ENGINE ECONOMY

*"The days of SEO being a game outsmarting algorithms are over. Today content strategy and valuable, sustainable strategies are essential, not just tricks and links."*

Adam Audette, Merkle RKG

## A Crash Course in Search Engines

As the name implies, search engines are powerful online programs that search for all kinds of information online. They perform three specific functions — crawling, indexing, and ranking. They "crawl" the Internet to identify the content available, and they build an index of this content. Then, based on user queries, the indexed content is ranked using a set of complex, top-secret parameters known as a search engine algorithm.

An algorithm is nothing more than a formula for solving a problem. In this case, a search engine's main problem is how to *rank* content.

The main service provided by companies like Google, Bing, and DuckDuckGo is to find the content users are searching for with the greatest possible accuracy, speed, quality, and relevance. They use algorithms to determine which sites are best matched to people's search terms and queries.

Link structures on the Internet bind all of these web pages together. Links — as in, clickable links that take you from one web page or website to another — are like the paths these *crawlers* walk down when performing their in-depth investigations. There are billions of pages to be crawled. These crawlers are constantly devouring link paths throughout the Internet and recording what they find in colossal databases.

 In the old days, some five or so years ago (which is like fifty in Google years), link building drove the SEO services industry. Link building is the process of getting third-party websites to place a clickable link (a.k.a. backlink) back to your website. While link building is still an important SEO tactic, many link building techniques have been outlawed or devalued by Google and other search engines because people used them to trick the system.

Today, link building takes a back seat to more holistic and sustainable approaches to ranking your website. The search engines are also much better at discerning natural backlinks from artificial ones.

Baidu, Yahoo, Yandex, and Bing are among the largest search engines in the world.[4] But none of these have been able to rival the market share or trailblazing nature of *Google* — the world's most dominant search engine.

## Googling's Gone Global

"Just google it" is one of the most common phrases you are likely to hear across the world these days. Why? Because Google won the search engine race, back when all of the search engines were vying for prominence in a burgeoning new field. From the moment the Internet went mainstream, there was a need to make more sense of it.

In 1995, most search terms returned illogical and sporadic results.[5] By 1997, a couple of Stanford University students decided to fix that problem. In 1998, one of those students, Google co-founder Larry Page, managed to outsmart earlier search engine technology by analyzing link relationships between websites. Instead of focusing on a web page's text, Google's algorithm calculated the relevance of a web page by looking at the volume and importance of the other web pages on the Internet linking back to that page. It cut the clutter and delivered remarkably accurate results. Google quickly rose to prominence and overwhelmed its competitors, sealing its destiny to become the search engine giant that it is now.

Today, Google is so much more than a search engine or a successful tech company. Its search technology is now a core part of the Internet and its digital infrastructure, as well as a fundamental component of the global economy.

---

4    Desktop Search Engine Market Share. http://marketshare.hitslink.com/search-engine-market-share.aspx?qprid=4&qpcustomd=0&qpcustom=

5    Tom Hormby, The Rise of Google: Beating Yahoo at Its Own Game, http://lowendmac.com/2013/the-rise-of-google-beating-yahoo-at-its-own-game/

Remember when Al Gore used to call the Internet, "the information superhighway?"[6] Well, it didn't quite turn out that way. If you think about it, Google has become the highway and content has become the destination. We all travel through Google and *its* indexed version of the Internet in order to get the information we want. The phrase "googling something" is now synonymous with "searching the Internet for it." This, in turn, has made Google an essential cog in the purchase process for virtually all online **business-to-customer (B2C)** and **business-to-business (B2B)** transactions. In simpler terms, Google decides which companies rise to Internet prominence, and which do not rise at all.

Consider Millward Brown Digital's 2014 survey of 3,000 B2B buyers:

- 89% of B2B researchers use the Internet during the B2B research process
- 71% of B2B researchers start their research with a generic search engine search
- 42% of B2B researchers use a mobile device during the B2B purchasing process
- 46% of B2B researchers are millennials[7]

A company or start-up that excels online today has done so by following Google's blueprint for what makes an online business relevant, trustworthy, and appealing to consumers. The search process not only has an impact on marketing, it is shaping parts of the economy.

Let's face it, Google is pretty much a monopoly. Their ever-evolving algorithm has made and lost fortunes for people over the last two decades. With the simple click of an update button, Google can reshuffle billions of search results in an instant, creating a new list of winners and losers. If you want your business or your web design customers to thrive online, then you cannot ignore SEO.

---

6    Remarks Prepared For Delivery By Vice President Al Gore, http://www.ibiblio.org/icky/speech2.html

7    https://www.thinkwithgoogle.com/articles/the-changing-face-b2b-marketing.html

The more you understand Google, the better you will be at search engine optimization. The two are interlinked because SEO grew directly from that company. So while SEO technically includes other search engines, it might as well be called Google optimization.

## Ranking Your Way to Success

SEO is as important to Google as it is for the rest of us. The vast majority of Google's revenue is derived from *AdWords*, its *pay-per-click (PPC)* and *cost-per-thousand-impressions (CPM)* advertising system.[8] Its business model is largely dependent on luring users from the *organic search results* to the paid advertising sections at the top of the search result pages.

QUICK TIP

For powerful search engine marketing, you need to take advantage of organic SEO for your website and consider supplementing your SEO campaign with pay-per-click (PPC) advertising on the AdWords platform. You can't rank organically for all keywords, and PPC can help you fill in those visibility gaps. Your AdWords account is also a great source of keyword data from Google. This two-pronged strategy will result in more targeted traffic to your website.

Depending on who you ask, only about 10-30% of Google users actually click on its PPC ads, with the vast majority preferring to click on organic search results. People do not go to Google to see its advertisements, they want natural search results. Internet users trust

---

8    http://www.investopedia.com/articles/investing/020515/business-google.asp

Google to consistently serve accurate results. According to data from 2016, some 5.5 billion searches are performed every day.[9] That's around 65,000 searches *per second*.

Like it or not, consumers associate high organic Google rankings with merit, ability, reputation, and trust. Whereas once upon a time, any old website could land on the first page of Google with minimal effort, it's not so easy these days. The truth is that 95% of users do not bother going past the first page of their search result.[10] This means that websites dominating this space get more traffic and *"**warm leads**"* — and even direct phone calls and email inquiries — as a result of a Google search than do businesses on page two and beyond.

SEO service providers target the first page of Google because roughly 40% of all traffic clicks on the first result immediately beneath the PPC ads.[11] This rate gradually falls with position two, three, and down through the rest of the page. So, even if you make it onto page one, a company ranked just two places above yours could get substantially more of those coveted warm leads than you.

Aside from these tasty stats, when you take into account that over 80% of all online buying decisions begin with an Internet search,[12] SEO becomes so much more than just a method of ranking well among your competitors. Bottom line: you need to get users to find your company online before you can convince them to buy anything from you.

---

9   Search Engine Land, http://searchengineland.com/google-now-handles-2-999-trillion-searches-per-year-250247

10  Barry Schwartz. A New Click Through Rate Study For Google Organic Results. http://marketingland.com/new-click-rate-study-google-organic-results-102149

11  Jeff Bullas, 10 Facts Reveal The Importance of Ranking In Google, http://www.jeffbullas.com/2010/07/14/10-facts-reveal-the-importance-of-ranking-high-in-google/

12  Kimberlee Morrison. 81% of Shoppers Conduct Online Research Before Buying [Infographic]. http://www.adweek.com/socialtimes/81-shoppers-conduct-online-research-making-purchase-infographic/208527

Google and the other search engines have become the modern equivalent of telephone directories on steroids. No one uses anything else these days to search for products and services. How many of us take phone directories directly from the door step to the recycle bin?

Googling has become such a common-place method of obtaining accurate information that even traditional referrals have changed. Now, when a friend or business acquaintance recommends someone to you, the next step is not to call them, but to Google them first! Search has become the crutch on which we all depend to make intelligent purchasing decisions.

With referrals in the firing line, it is no wonder that more people are paying attention to SEO than ever before. If you have no presence on Google, you don't exist in the digital world. And if you don't have a professional online presence, you probably aren't converting as much referral business as you should be.

With the right SEO techniques, you can rank your way into new revenue streams and a greater market share. That is not just a fact; it is a modern day marvel. Many successful companies and brands already know that effective SEO produces a killer ROI, and they dedicate time and resources accordingly. Whether you are a one-man band or the CEO of a large company, you can get the same results too.

## The Future of SEO

SEO is in a constant state of flux. It has grown from the tricks of the early 2000s into a much more mature, content-driven concern. And it will continue to evolve as Google and other search companies develop and enhance the technology to help people find the best solutions for their online queries.

SEO is no longer about tweaking keywords and getting *backlinks*.[13] Google expects you to be a content machine. They want you to demonstrate your expertise and authority by investing in high-quality

---

13  Marcus Sheridan, Google 2015, http://www.thesaleslion.com/future-google-seo-2015/

content that your ideal customers want to consume. They also want to see your content being engaged and shared via social media. This is why, to rank well on Google, you need to be creating and distributing a variety of content all the time.

**Fresh, original, and relevant content is the best form of value that you can deliver to your search users.** What your potential customers want most is a reason to choose you over other companies. They want to see strong organic rankings backed by quality website content, active social media communities, and positive customer reviews in order to confidently make you their choice.

Content is not only king, it's the most important of all Google ranking factors. Over the last few years, Google has made this abundantly clear with the purpose and focus of its algorithm updates. It wants SEO to be a natural process of content creation and delivery.

Google is taking a holistic view of the Internet and how people use it to make decisions. Features like transparency, honesty, integrity, and entertainment will become more important — and the time of "SEO experts" will pass. Content marketing experts are already taking their place.

The future of SEO, friends, is not about tricks and tweaks; it's about creating great content on a regular basis. Quality and user engagement will be the hallmarks of sites that rank well in the future. If you can adopt these principles now, you will be in a prime position to win big as Google continues on this path.

## Creating vs. Capturing Demand

There is a tug of war in marketing and advertising right now. There are two general styles that determine a company's cost of customer acquisition and overall return on investment: the older, *outbound* tactic of *demand creation* and the newer *inbound* methods of *demand capture*.

With *demand creation*, marketers focus on creating new sales via various forms of outbound marketing and mass-market advertising.

They try to spur sales from people who are not on the purchase path. Successful demand creators are typically creative and imaginative, but can also be aggressive and annoying. They use TV, radio, direct mail, cold-calling, and phone directory advertising to reach a large audience with the hopes of selling to a fraction of those they reach. Seth Godin refers to some of their tactics as "interruption marketing," that is, advertising to people by interrupting them while they are doing something they enjoy or while they are working.

Traditional creative agencies and advertising agencies still focus on selling big-dollar demand-creation services, while clever search engine marketers use pennies to snatch away these purchases online. It drives big agencies crazy that nameless, brandless companies can leverage such a small budget to generate so much new business.

With demand capture, marketers focus on harvesting demand created by other companies. SEO is all about catching buyers when they are already in the purchase process, while at the same time leveraging the marketing dollars of your competition. In other words, a person may be inspired to fix a plumbing issue when he sees a plumbing commercial (demand creation), but he will likely follow up on that inspiration with an Internet search to find and choose the best service provider (demand capture). With SEO, you let your competitors do all the expensive, low-ROI advertising while you position your company to steal that demand as it filters through the Internet.

It is your job as an online marketer to become a superstar at capturing demand on the Internet. It is not enough to get that first click. You have to convince readers to buy, come back, and buy again.

In the search engine economy, demand capture is where most small businesses should focus today. The vast majority of your potential customers are searching for your products and services right now. The only thing preventing many of them from buying from you is the fact that you don't pop up on Google for the right search terms.

## Expert to Watch: *Danny Sullivan*

Danny Sullivan is one of the original SEO experts who started reporting on search engine optimization back in 1997, even before Google was a household name. He coined the term "*search engine marketing*" (SEM) and has been a major player in the SEO industry for many years.

Danny is the Chief Content Officer at Third Door Media, a title which underscores how closely content marketing and SEO are intertwined right now. He is most well known for his writing on two of the most prominent SEO websites running today, which he co-founded and grew into industry giants: Search Engine Land and its sister site, Marketing Land. These websites cover news and information on SEO and SEM, as well as social media, online advertising, email marketing, analytics, and emerging technology.

Third Door Media, which Danny co-owns, also runs the Digital Marketing Depot, an online resource center for digital marketing strategies and tactics, where you can find excellent webcasts and webinars that are available both live and on demand to members.

Third Door Media also operates two prominent industry conferences: The Search Marketing Expo, one of the world's most popular search engine marketing conferences and The Marketing Tech Conference, which showcases marketing technologies and up-and-coming technologies that could impact the realm of marketing in the future.

Danny began his early career as a journalist working for the Los Angeles Times and the Orange County Register, perfectly positioning him to later begin reporting on search engines and technology during

SEO's rise. Although today Danny takes more of a managerial role than a writing one, he continues to break stories and provide thought leadership for the industry.

We highly recommend that you follow Danny on Twitter @ dannysullivan and make a habit of reading both Search Engine Land[14] and Marketing Land.[15] These sites provide a macro-level view of the SEO industry and will keep you up to date on news that you can trust. They have been paramount in maintaining our own industry knowledge, as they are always the first to report when something has happened or fundamentally changed in the niche. With so many self-proclaimed experts in the world of SEO, it pays to know which sources provide the best information.

---

14  About Search Engine Land, http://searchengineland.com/about

15  About Marketing Land, http://marketingland.com/about

# THE GOOGLE
# ALGORITHM TODAY

*"It is no coincidence that the increasing focus on content marketing closely follows the significant Google algorithmic changes aiming to give users a better search experience."*

Jim Yu, Brightedge

Ah yes, the Google algorithm . . . a terrifying, ever-changing creature that can be a total nightmare if you do not track and analyze its movements all the time. For many years, Google updated its algorithm and nothing major changed for SEO service providers who continued working to game the system.

Then, a few years ago, the entire game changed. New punitive algorithm updates were released, and they sent the industry into panic. Even Fortune 500 brands were affected. The days of handing an SEO company a check every month and expecting to rank on the first page with back-room SEO tactics are over.

## The Age of the Algorithm

We live in the age of the algorithm, where the entire SEO industry revolves around Google and how it chooses ranking winners. Each year, Google adjusts its algorithm about 500-600 times,[16] making minute changes that can have varying effects on daily search results.

Every now and then, Google releases a major update — a large, forceful, and prominent algorithm update that changes SEO forever. This is what makes the SEO industry so volatile, so unpredictable, and so wonderfully exciting. These changes to organic search are the bread and butter of people in the search engine marketing business.

**QUICK TIP**

It goes without saying that if you do not know what has changed, you do not know your industry. There is no resting on laurels for SEO. When a major update happens, prepare to sink into study, to figure out how it may impact your website properties. Ignoring these can be harmful to your website visibility.

Major updates began in the early 2000s in order to curb aggressive webmasters from manipulating search engine results and to make search more accurate, trustworthy, and predictable for the searcher.

In January 2011, Google outed Overstock.com for "bad behavior," which included compensating students and faculty members at universities with discounts in exchange for linking to Overstock's website.[17] This public outing for shady link building practices marked a

---

16  Google Algorithm Change History. https://moz.com/google-algorithm-change

17  Amir Efrati. Google Penalizes Overstock for Search Tactics. http://www.wsj.com/articles/SB10001424052748704520504576162753779521700

major shift at Google and a new algorithmic focus to penalize websites that violate their quality guidelines.

Another example can be found in 2014, when eBay lost 33% of all online traffic as a result of a Google algorithm update.[18] It must have cost eBay a pretty penny before it could adjust. Being informed and proactive is your best defense against future updates.

In the age of the algorithm, you cannot expect a cold-calling SEO company to provide you with "guaranteed results". You can no longer pay these companies for link building short-cuts and *black hat SEO* techniques. Google expects you to follow the rules, and it is enforcing them with a vengeance.

## Google Penguin and Panda

As mentioned, there have been major changes to the Google algorithm that have had a significant impact on websites all over the world. [19] Perhaps the most drastic and unnerving updates were Penguin and Panda. Many websites were heavily penalized by each of these updates for spammy and manipulative SEO practices. Even some large brands dropped off their top spots for a time.

The first of these game-changers was Google's Panda update, named after Navneet Panda, one of its creators. Released on February 23, 2011, Panda was meant to boost higher quality sites in the search results and to demote sites that contained low-quality and duplicate content, as well as "thin" web pages with very little content and of low value to users.

Spammy *"content farms"* were immediately hit by Panda. These websites aggregated information from many different places online, or they simply stole other websites' content and tried to pass it off as their own. The goal of these websites was to trick Google by creating many pages of content for the sole purpose of gaining rank for a wide variety

---

18  Dr. Peter.J.Meyers. Panda 4.0, Payday Loan 2.0 & eBay's Very Bad Day. https://moz.com/blog/panda-4-payday-loan-2-and-ebays-very-bad-day

19  2011 Updates, https://moz.com/google-algorithm-change#2011

of keywords, rather than adding value to users. Often these content farms would earn big money in advertising or affiliate marketing revenue.

Although content farms were the worst hit, many other websites also tanked because of poor content and on-page SEO practices. *On-page SEO* refers to many types of ranking factors on your website such as the text content, website coding, and the navigation structure of your site. *Off-page SEO* refers to a wide range of ranking factors external to your website such as backlinks and social media signals. The day Panda launched, many SEO experts thought that questionable backlinking practices were to blame, but as it turned out, Panda was never about anything but on-site content quality.

More specifically, Panda targets sites with duplicate content, copied content, too many and/or irrelevant keywords (known as *keyword stuffing*), similar "mass" articles reworked for ranking purposes, unreliable information, information written by non-subject matter experts, content with obvious grammatical errors, and unoriginal content.

On the whole, you have to make sure each web page contains sufficient information, that there is minimal duplication across your website, and that all of your site content is original and meets a high standard worthy of any print publication.

The Penguin update caused similar problems for webmasters on April 24, 2012. [20] Penguin's goal was to reduce Google's trust in sites using unnatural backlinking practices in order to gain prominence in the search results. While Penguin targets various off-page factors, this infamous updated targeted *inbound links* — an element on a third-party website leading back to your website via a clickable link.

When a credible website links to yours, it acts as a vote of confidence, which signals to Google that your site is high quality. In the past, getting

---

20  Difference Between Google Panda and Google Penguin, http://seoupdates.info/difference-between-google-panda-and-google-penguin/

many links from small, unknown sites had the same effect as getting a few links from top-authority sites. As a result, many SEO service providers would engage in volume-based link building activities that violated Google's quality guidelines. Know the guys who are cold-calling or robocalling your business and spamming your email on SEO services? Most of them are still selling low-quality link building services.

Penguin aggressively targets keyword-rich *anchor text*. Anchor text is a clickable **word** or **phrase** that links to another web page. Google scrutinizes these types of links, so using them to manipulate *search engine rankings* is very risky. At the same time, links are still a <u>very</u> important ranking factor and helpful for SEO when they are a natural fit and add editorial value to web page content. In fact, Google explicitly tells people to "make sure that other sites link to yours:"

**https://support.google.com/webmasters/answer/40349**

With each new Penguin update, Google gets better at finding and assessing the value and purpose of backlinks and rewarding or penalizing sites accordingly.

To make sure that your websites are not at risk for the next Penguin update, make sure that your link building practices are genuine, and pay close attention to the quality and relevance of third-party sites linking back to you.

## Google Hummingbird, RankBrain, and Pigeon

One of the biggest updates of all time wasn't really an update' it was a dramatic rewrite of the entire algorithm. Hummingbird affected more than 90% of all searches,[21] which means that the results for billions of daily search queries were reshuffled.

Hummingbird became known as the update that focused on context and semantics. Focusing on a "semantic search" means improving

---

21 Jeremy Hull. Google Hummingbird: Where No Search Has Gone Before. http://www.wired.com/insights/2013/10/google-hummingbird-where-no-search-has-gone-before/

search results by thinking about what the user intends to find instead of matching individual keywords to web page copy. In other words, this update focuses on contextual relevance.

Hummingbird marked Google's first step toward incorporating artificial intelligence into search, in this case to help computers understand differences in context and intention. In 2015, Google announced that its machine-learning system, "Rank Brain," was working in conjunction with Hummingbird to produce more meaningful search results. Today, Rank Brain is a top organic ranking factor.

A Knowledge Box, an example of a semantic search result, kicks in when you want to search for things like the local weather. [22] When one types "local weather" into Google, the search engine assumes you are searching for the temperature in your area and provides you with the answer; you don't have to click a thing. Rather than giving you a list of options through which you may find the answer on third-party websites, Google now attempts to provide it to you directly in the search results through "rich answers" in the form of Knowledge Graphs, Knowledge Panels and answer boxes. This information is typically delivered via an information box at the top or on the right of the search results page. Of course, other results are still listed if it turns out you were looking for something else.

 **QUICK TIP** It is reasonable to assume that Google will improve its Knowledge Graph and other direct content features, which means that your site content will have to be extra good to qualify for visibility on Google. Focus on enriching your user's experience and creating top-quality content from this day forward.

---

22  Dan Shewan, How Google Hummingbird Changed The Future of Search, http://www. wordstream.com/blog/ws/2014/06/23/google-hummingbird

Google Pigeon was another notable update, this time having do with local search. The algorithm was updated to provide more useful, relevant, and accurate local results in web search rankings.

In short, Pigeon connected Google web search results more directly to map search results. The best thing about Pigeon, however, is that traditional search engine ranking factors now affect local search results. This means that you can improve your map search result potential with best-practices SEO. Many companies may have noticed either a dip in their local referral traffic from Google search or a significant Pigeon windfall, depending on a variety of factors such as site content and proactive online reputation management.

## Working Above the Fold

In 2012 Matt Cutts, Google's de facto SEO spokesman until 2014, announced an update to the algorithm called the Page Layout update that would, from then on, demote the rank of websites without enough relevant content "above the fold," or before a viewer had to scroll down on the screen.

This update stemmed from Google's obsession with optimizing *user experience*. Users want to find their content quickly — they don't want to have to scroll through ads and other complications for ten minutes before they can locate the answer to their search query. So, to encourage webmasters *and web designers* to rethink their page layouts and ad placements, Google launched the above the fold update.

As a result, websites with loads of ads and no valuable content above the fold rank lower in the search results. When designing or redesigning a new website for your business or client, this is an important point to remember.

In SEO, "above the fold" now refers to anything that a user sees when they land on your web page for the first time, without any scrolling action.[23] The location of all of your images, text, ads, forms, and videos

---

23  Tim Allen, Life Above and Beyond The Fold, https://moz.com/blog/life-above-and-beyond-the-fold

on a web page will affect how Google values that page. Optimizing this very important space can improve your search engine ranking potential.

**QUICK TIP**

Put yourself in the user's shoes when designing the "above the fold" space on your website. Your website needs to make a positive impression immediately, and you only have a few seconds after that to convince visitors that your website offers a solution to their problem. The core message should jump off the top of the page, especially your home page. Consider placing a very clear *call to action* above the fold as well, so that you have the best possible chance of converting each and every new visitor into a sale, inquiry, follower, or subscriber.

While users have become much more accustomed to scrolling, content above the fold is still very important for website conversions. As a web designer or business owner, you should carefully design this area to maximize value. Consider limiting the amount of ads and graphics that you put above the fold and be sure to include your most important messaging at, or towards, the top of your home page. When you structure articles, web pages, or blog posts, you should also consider creating a layout that delivers the best information at the top of your page.

If you want a more accurate reading of how your users consume your website content, we strongly suggest using a heat map tool such as Crazy Egg:

**http://www.crazyegg.com**

Designing your website to take advantage of this space will ultimately improve your SEO potential.

## HTTPS and Mobile-Friendly

The algorithm updates have been coming fast and furious over the last five years, as Google's definition of a quality website continues to evolve. Another example is a security-related update that gave preference to sites with "https connections" over sites without them. You know you are connected to an SSL-enabled site when you see the familiar green bar in the browser bar with https:// at the start or the page URL instead of a plain old http:// connection. For example:

**http://seoforgrowth.com**

**vs.**

**https://seoforgrowth.com**

To qualify for the extra https ranking points, all you have to do is properly install an SSL certificate. This will also provide your users with additional added transaction, browsing, and personal protection. The update comes in the wake of user concerns regarding privacy and security while web browsing. You can test your SSL installation here:

**https://www.ssllabs.com/ssltest/**

There are some technical SEO considerations with respect to converting an existing http site to https, so you may want to consult an experienced professional before implementing this change. It is a lightweight ranking signal as far as Google updates go, affecting only 1% of global search traffic,[24] so for now, it does not bear nearly as much weight as other ranking factors like quality content. That said, it is

---

24  Google Webmaster Central Blog. HTTPS as a ranking signal. http://googlewebmastercentral.blogspot.com/2014/08/https-as-ranking-signal.html

likely that SSL-enabled sites will be standard in the future, and SEO experts project more security-related updates from Google.[25] Even Matt Cutts has been quoted as saying that he would like security to have more weight in the algorithm. So if you have the budget, establishing a secure connection to your website may be a strong SEO move.

Yet another big change to hit search was the mobile-friendly update, referred to by some experts as "Mobilegeddon." This update made waves not only for its substance, but because of the way in which it was announced: ahead of time and with a specific launch date, both of which were unprecedented in the world of SEO.

In 2015, there were more searches on mobile devices than on desktops in the US and Japan.[26] Google had warned webmasters for years to make web pages mobile-compliant so users could easily browse on a mobile device. That warning became official as of April 21, 2015, when Google started giving mobile-friendly pages get a ranking boost. In other words, Google says your website has to be mobile-friendly. Period.

Google also warned that when all is said and done, the mobile-friendly update would impact more websites than Panda and Penguin combined. To this day, many businesses miss out on opportunities to generate web traffic because they have not addressed their websites' mobile issues. The future of the Internet is tied directly to mobile technology. Google understands this better than anyone, because it's the one making it happen.

You can test if your website is mobile-friendly here:

**https://www.google.com/webmasters/tools/mobile-friendly/**

---

25  Darah Perez, Google's Mobile Friendly Update Could Impact Over 40% of Fortune 500 Websites, http://techcrunch.com/2015/04/21/googles-mobile-friendly-update-could-impact-over-40-of-fortune-500/#.fqnm6k:GqPe

26  Greg Sterling. It's Official: Google Says More Searches Now On Mobile Than On Desktop. http://searchengineland.com/its-official-google-says-more-searches-now-on-mobile-than-on-desktop-220369)

In October of 2015, Google announced yet another mobile-search improvement: Accelerated Mobile Pages (AMP).[27] The goal of this new open-source initiative is to improve performance of the mobile web. Google has also mentioned more than once that AMP is likely to become a direct organic ranking factor.

## Penalties and Manual Actions

Google continues to update its algorithm to make technologies, such as Penguin and Panda, faster and more effective. There are also dozens of other algorithm updates that have shaped SEO, and these will affect your website in the coming years.

For a comprehensive list of Google updates since 2000, see:

**https://moz.com/google-algorithm-change**

Here are a few other algorithm updates and how they have affected Google Search:

- **The Exact Match Domain Update**: This affected websites with keyword terms in their domains, but poor quality content on their sites. Google no longer ranks a domain well for a keyword just because it's part of the main URL. In other words, having a great keyword-rich domain name is no longer the SEO silver bullet it once was (although it still seems to help).
- **The Pirate Update**: This filter prevents sites with many copyright infringement reports from ranking well on the search engine. Google penalizes websites that break copyright laws.
- **The Payday Loan Update**: Launched in 2013, this update aimed to clean up search results for traditionally spammy queries like "payday loans" and other very heavily spammed niches. If you operate within one of these niches, you can thank this update for giving you the chance to rank well with content-driven SEO.

---

27 https://googleblog.blogspot.com/2015/10/introducing-accelerated-mobile-pages.html.

Aside from automated algorithmic penalties, Google takes *manual action* on sites that use spammy SEO techniques by demoting them or even removing them altogether from search results. This typically happens when a site is flagged for abusing Google's quality guidelines. A person at Google will physically assign a penalty to your website. Some people refer to this as being "blacklisted."

The good news is that Google always notifies you of *manual penalties* in Google Search Console (formerly Webmaster Tools). This provides you with an opportunity to review your site and fix the problem, which you can then resubmit to Google to get you back in the game.

## https://www.google.com/webmasters/

Websites often incur penalties because of algorithm updates or when they get caught using black hat SEO techniques. We cannot emphasize this enough: Google is wise to the spammy SEO techniques that once worked, and it will penalize your site and maybe even *deindex* your website (i.e., completely remove your site from Google) if its algorithms catch you trying to take prohibited SEO shortcuts. Cold-calling and robocalling SEO companies offering link building packages are not worth the risk. In the end, the search engines always find you and make you pay the price. It's far more beneficial to invest in legitimate SEO tactics than to waste time with techniques that will come back to bite you.

Some websites still find ways to benefit from SEO shortcuts. For example, the unintended consequence of the Penguin update was negative SEO.[28] Since Penguin is a punitive algorithm that targets volume-based link building, some people have tried driving low-quality links to competing websites in order to trigger a Penguin penalty or a manual action. This may be the dirtiest form of black hat SEO. It is one thing to cheat by taking performance-enhancing drugs, but it's another

---

28   Rand Fishkin, How To Handle a Google Penalty – And An Example From The Field of Real Estate, https://moz.com/blog/how-to-handle-a-google-penalty-and-an-example-from-the-field-of-real-estate

to try to break your competitor's leg. Subsequent Penguin updates seem to have greatly reduced the effectiveness of negative SEO, but many experts believe it is still a clear and present danger. This is why managing your website's backlink profile on a regular basis is part of modern SEO. You need to be earning high-quality, relevant links from authority websites, but you also need to be consistently pruning bad links from your site. There is even a link disavow tool and process that can help you manage unwanted backlinks in Google Search Console.

The moral of the story is that Google wants the best because its users demand the best. You have to follow the rules of the all-knowing, all-seeing algorithm, or you will pay for it sooner or later. If you play fair and focus on best practices SEO, it is unlikely that you will ever have to worry about the types of penalties discussed in this chapter.

## Expert to Watch: *Barry Schwartz*

One of the top SEO guys in our industry is Barry Schwartz.[29] He is the CEO of RustyBrick, a New York web services firm that specializes in website and app development. Barry is also the news editor at Danny Sullivan's Search Engine Land.

Barry's most notable claim to fame is his popular Search Engine Roundtable, which has been running for over a decade. This is a very special website and our personal favorite for staying on top of algorithm updates and other search engine changes affecting SEO. Barry uses it to aggregate SEO chatter from forums and other community sites about how changes are affecting websites *right now* and conveys it in daily, easy-to-read blog posts. Since Google rarely announces algorithm updates, Search Engine Roundtable is the best industry website from which to get real-time information on Google updates.

Barry's career began, like Danny Sullivan's, by blogging about search engine marketing. Barry has also written extensively for Search Engine Watch, another prominent SEO website. He has invested a lot of time

---

29  Barry Schwartz CEO of RustyBrick, https://www.rustybrick.com/barry

creating unique information about SEO for many prominent online publications. It is not uncommon to find him quoted in SEO books, appearing as a guest expert on television shows and online webinars, or moderating a top-level forum. He has also written important thought-leadership posts that have been published on the websites of *Forbes*, the *Wall Street Journal*, the *New York Times,* and *USA Today.*

Barry has spoken at dozens of SEO conferences and industry events over the years, including PubCon, Search Engine Strategies, and SEMSEO in Germany, where he was the keynote speaker. He has also hosted a radio show called *The Pulse* at WebmasterRadio.FM.

As an industry leader, Barry's online profile is worth adding to your list so you are always up to date on what is going on with the Google algorithm. It is a good idea to follow Barry's news feed on Search Engine Land and to follow all of his social media platforms, where he regularly delivers the latest news and insights. Barry has well over 100,000 followers on Google+, where he posts interesting videos and curates some of the best SEO posts from all around the Internet.

SEO has many important voices, so following several prominent industry experts, such as Barry on Twitter @rustybrick, will ensure that you get the whole story when updates are released.

# THE INBOUND MARKETING SUPER-WEAPON

*"People shop and learn in a whole new way compared to just a few years ago, so marketers need to adapt or risk extinction."*

Brian Halligan, Hubspot

There is a super weapon in the marketing landscape today. It combines the unique practices of SEO and social media, uniting in a web-centric system that attracts potential customers, fans, and advocates to your brand.

The *inbound marketing* method is how online businesses convert random strangers into long-term, loyal customers. Using a deliberate blend of digital marketing techniques, this method has all but replaced traditional forms of *outbound marketing*.

## The Inbound Marketing Arena

Inbound marketing is the most effective form of marketing in today's digital age. It attracts, educates, and converts new customers using different online touchpoints that are part of a brand's online presence. The older outbound marketing style of previous decades is fading away. The ROI from buying advertising, email lists, print pamphlets, cold-calling, television, radio ads, and other forms of mass-marketing isn't what it used to be. Inbound marketing draws customers to your doorstep, and it can bring them in droves.

By aligning the content that you publish with your customers' interests, you attract the people that are most likely to buy from your company. [30] The keystone of this methodology is creating quality and diverse forms of content to share on the Internet. Inbound marketing helps you publish the right content, at the right time, in the right place.

 In digital marketing, a call to action (CTA) is an instruction on your website designed to provoke users into entering the path to conversion. Your website CTAs should be clearly visible, above the fold, and include a unique and compelling offer that draws visitors into your inbound marketing system before they exist your site.

When ideal clients first visit your website, you want them to take one of five actions before leaving: buy, try, call, email, or follow. With inbound marketing, there are three key tactical areas you need to attract visitors, build an audience, and convert them to sales:

- You need to build a great website with a *blog* that consistently delivers deliberate, full optimized quality content. You also need

---

30  The Inbound Methodology, http://www.hubspot.com/inbound-marketing

to actively participate in social media channels and establish a footprint.

- To convert new website visitors, you need to capture their details with *calls to action*, online forms, and *landing pages*. Creative sales copy coupled with compelling graphic design and call to action carrots (such as free eBooks or special discount offers), will help spur the desired action. You will build a marketing database of emails that will become a key asset in this process.

- With inbound marketing, it is imperative that you delight your consumers. This involves customer relationship management, closed-loop reporting, and email and marketing automation. Surveys, social monitoring, analytics, and smart content creation are also important elements of the system.

## The Future is Content Marketing

Within the inbound marketing sphere, another, more direct, form of digital marketing has replaced link building in terms of focus and importance in the SEO industry — content marketing.

Content marketing can be defined as a strategic marketing approach that focuses on creating and distributing valuable, relevant, and consistent content to attract and retain a clearly defined audience, who, in turn, will drive profitable customer action. [31] In terms of SEO, a properly executed content marketing strategy will naturally attract the best kind of backlinks and genuine social signals.

Content can influence customer behavior over time. As an ongoing process, content marketing is the art and science of effectively communicating with your audience, so that you can sell your products with enough predictability to grow your business.

Unlike many other types of marketing, content marketing does not directly sell your products or services. There are very few direct

---

31  What Is Content Marketing, http://contentmarketinginstitute.com/what-is-content-marketing/

marketing messages in this discipline. When you market with content, you aim to entertain, educate, or enhance the information surrounding your business. In other words, **teaching is the new marketing**.

Content is the present and the future of marketing.[32] If you infuse your content with your brand's story and help your consumers understand what you believe in and why, they will choose to buy from you. This is what makes content marketing such a highly effective form of marketing.

A strong piece of content might make someone stop, read, think, and then take action. An educational video created by a natural health company on the dangers of sugar is a good example. It can include modern research and information that would enrich the users' search experience. If the user decides she trusts the brand, she will naturally click over to her list of natural supplements to purchase some Stevia. At no point in the video did the company overtly advertise its products, because the focus was on the user and education, not the marketing message. Modern consumers love this form of media because it is non-intrusive and leaves the choice to them.

The key variable in content marketing is *value*. This is why it aligns well with the Google algorithm, because the two work hand in hand to deliver a better experience to the end user. Any form of content can be part of a content marketing campaign, and you should be aware that there is an extensive range of mediums available.

From podcasts, web pages, *blog* posts, and videos to landing pages, books, tweets, Facebook posts, and guest webinars, content fuels SEO like wood fuels a fire.

## The Authority Marketplace

Content marketing has become the most effective way to gain authority

---

32  Joshua Steimle, What Is Content Marketing, http://www.forbes.com/sites/joshsteimle/2014/09/19/what-is-content-marketing/

in today's marketplace. [33] With the right content, you can soft-sell anything to a targeted audience, saving you time, money, and effort. All you need is a strong strategy, an SEO mindset, and the ability to consistently create high-quality content.

In today's authority marketplace, the companies with the best content become the most respected. This also signals to Google, through visits and engagement, that you are a subject-matter expert. Use content marketing to build authority in your niche, and you will dramatically improve your website's online visibility.

A business that spends time building authority and subject-matter expertise can dominate its niche. Many brands have done this in order to leapfrog over their competition. They publish expert posts in their niche and have become the "go-to" teachers, mentors, and experts because of it.

Anyone can brand herself an expert, but it takes meticulous strategy, high-quality content, and consistency to convince Google that the expertise is authentic. [34] Brands or personalities that are the most searched are the ones making the most money. Google leads by example by periodically releasing free courses and webinars, and by regular old blog posts.

---

33 Brian Honigman, How To Use Content Marketing To Build Authority and Subject Matter Expertise, http://www.skyword.com/contentstandard/art-of-storytelling/how-to-use-content-marketing-to-build-authority-and-subject-matter-expertise/

34 What Is Content Authority, https://www.marketingtechblog.com/what-is-content-authority/

There has been an explosion in image and video content over the last five years, but nothing beats good, solid text. Writing is a critical element for lending weight, trust, and credibility to your brand. A company with good writing resources can build a strong online following, which can be converted into repeat sales.

If you had capitalized on the content marketing trend back in 2010, your brand would be significantly larger today. Content marketing is here to stay, and it's never too late to get started. Just like backlinks, you need to focus on quality rather than quantity. If you start pumping out fluffy, useless content, your content marketing efforts will backfire. Keep in mind that the kind of content your company chooses to create will shape how customers perceive your brand online.

## Building Content Distribution Channels

A content distribution channel is any platform your brand can use to consistently publish content online. Multiple channels form a major network of your personalized brand content and should all point back to your website. In content marketing, your website is like the "central command" for all of your content.

You control your own destiny on your website, but not so on platforms like Facebook or Google+, where any small policy change might negatively impact your business. **You want your website to be the referral source for all of your best content.** It's much more beneficial, from an SEO standpoint, to post a story on your website's blog and then to share that post on Facebook, than it is to publish the content directly on Facebook with no digital trail back to your site. In other words, publish on your website, then share and distribute that content on social media.

SEO experts focus on building websites that rank. Business owners want quality online leads and for the phone to ring off the hook. To attain both of these, you need to understand how to build online content distribution channels. And it all starts with articulating your main goals and metrics, and then developing an overarching content strategy that will govern your individual channel strategies.

 Think of each channel point as a piece of your brand puzzle. Your content should not be the same on every platform, but rather should be tailored for that specific audience. Each channel will need to be optimized to suit the style and needs of that platform, according to what works best for that community. Remember that content posted in your distribution rainbow must lead back to your site to turn it into a lead-generating pot of gold.

You should think of content marketing in terms of a strategy,[35] not as a random marketing tactic. It encompasses all of your channels and lays out how they work in unison to build a complete picture for your user. Along with your website and blog, the other five main channels you should focus on are Facebook, LinkedIn, Google+, Twitter, and YouTube. There are many other social media channels that may be effective for your business, such as Pinterest and Instagram, as well as niche websites such as Houzz. If your customers are members of other social media websites, you need a presence on those too. Your content distribution channel should also include guest-blogging partnerships with third-party websites, online press release services, and any business or association website where you can reliably publish content or news about your business.

---

35  Developing a Content Marketing Strategy, http://contentmarketinginstitute.com/developing-a-strategy/

With your website at the core of your marketing pursuits, you will strike out and develop content distribution channels that will shape the face of your brand online. In terms of SEO, your custom channel will enable you to consistently distribute fresh content to an ever- growing audience. This, in turn, will generate social and website engagement signals that will contribute to higher search engine rankings.

## Blogs and Guest Blogging

Back in 2009, top content marketers realized that blogging was a powerful tool for SEO. Facebook was reaching an unfathomable level of popularity, and social media was shiny and new. Marketing pros that saw the potential in creating original content for SEO are now leaders in the field.

You can still replicate this success for your brand. A website with a blog is a powerful publication tool. Google essentially wants your company to open a publishing division and invest in creating great content for your brand. Its algorithm updates have made this very clear. Fresh, high-quality content regularly posted on a blog is a major ranking factor.

A business without a blog is a business looking for trouble. Credible companies need to realize that a single blog post each week on an optimized website will land them higher in the search rankings over time than will wasting money on low-quality SEO services on a static website.

Once your brand or a personality within your brand, has established a blog, you are a subject- matter expert. You can now engage in the industry's best- kept secret — guest blogging. The best bloggers in a specific niche tend to know each other, because they leverage one another for influencer marketing, social media amplification, and yes, SEO. [36]

---

36  Louis Gudema, How Guest Blogging Solved My SEO Problem, http:// contentmarketinginstitute.com/2015/02/guest-blogging-seo-problem/

**QUICK TIP** Guest blogging is a content marketing tactic. To do it right, you need to identify high-quality websites relevant to your industry. Your goal is to create an educational (non-advertorial) blog post and submit it to the site owner for publishing. Be sure to include a bio at the end of your guest blog post that includes a link to your website and at least one social media account. Upon publishing, both parties should cross-amplify the post in social media for maximum exposure. Guest blogging is unique in its ability to generate many levels of social media, marketing, and SEO value. Consider inviting guest bloggers to occasionally publish on your website as well.

Aside from killer content, what does Google love most? Genuine links! Guest blogging (for free, not paid) is one of the best possible methods of earning quality, genuine links that improve the credibility of your website. If you can create expert contributor posts for high quality, third-party websites relevant to your niche, you will get SEO value from them.

Guest blogging is a good way to show Google that your content is important and useful within your niche. It is not easy, and you will have to do some legwork and outreach to find guest blogging opportunities, but it is worth it.

Don't try to cheat Google by creating link-laden, keyword-stuffed, spammy content to publish on poor-quality websites. **Using guest blogging for the sole purpose of getting backlinks to your site is just another silly form of black hat SEO.** Create original, high-quality, niche information of which you are proud. This is how you can use guest blogging to grow your audience and make a positive contribution to your search engine rankings.

Website authority is about who links to you, and guest blogging typically results in links back to your website. As you strategically create and publish guest blog posts, these links will, over time, contribute to a well-rounded SEO strategy. While guest blogging is popular in the SEO niche, relatively few companies use this tactic, which leaves you with an opportunity on which to capitalize.

## Books, eBooks, Case Studies, and More

Valuable, optimized content is essential to content marketing, with diversity of formats being a key element. The companies that are winning big online are using digital content to build their authority and online brand presence. This is how you build an SEO wall that will be tough for your competitors to break. [37] We have discussed social media and blog posting at length, so here are other forms of content to add to your arsenal:

- *Print Books*: With many self-publishing options today, it's much easier to create and publish a book than you might think. Many brands are doing this now, and it not only helps you establish niche authority, but enables your brand to leverage the power of Amazon and other online book-distribution networks.

- *eBooks:* Create an eBook on a topic that will promote your products or services by telling a story or educating an audience. EBooks are used as lead magnets and subscriber incentives to build email lists, or they are sold on Amazon as an additional revenue source.

- *Case Studies*: These prove to your users that you have a track record of past successes. They can be posted on your website, shared on social media, and used in official marketing publications.

---

37  Neil Patel, 15 Types of Content That Will Drive You More Traffic, http://www. quicksprout.com/2014/04/14/how-these-15-types-of-content-will-drive-you-more-traffic/

- **Whitepapers**: Establish yourself as an industry expert by publishing periodic whitepapers on common problems and solutions in your field. Persuasive whitepapers are a clear demonstration of authority.

- **Infographics**: Infographics appeal to members of your audience who are more visual or have shorter attention spans. These detailed graphic images tell a story by laying out complex information in a simple format that is attractive to the eye. They are highly sharable and make excellent social media posts.

- **Web Videos**: Aside from blog posts, nothing beats video in terms of SEO and conversion value. Build trust and authority by creating how-to and explainer videos. Do reviews, talk about industry news, and work with your customers and strategic partners to create testimonial videos.

- **Webinars**: A webinar is a short online course that educates people on a specific subject. It usually includes a few subject-matter experts who discuss or explain something important. These can be live or they can be staged.

- **Slideshow Presentations:** Any time you use a PowerPoint presentation to present to an audience, be sure to upload that presentation to a slideshow-sharing site such as SlideShare.net. Once published, your presentations can achieve their own organic rank, and similar to videos, this media file can be embedded on third-party websites.

- **Guides and User Manuals**: Content can be instructive, and there is nothing more rewarding than educating your audience. A good guide not only tells your potential buyer how you do something, but why. These are great sales tools!

These and other content formats will help you feed the "content monster" that is born the moment you implement a content strategy. SEO relies on fresh, relevant content, so keep these forms of content coming!

## Expert to Watch: *Ann Handley*[38]

Ann Handley is the Chief Content Officer for MarketingProfs, a leading website with a large following that explores modern marketing techniques. She is a master of creating and managing digital strategies for organizations and brands, and she's a bestselling *Wall Street Journal* author to boot.

Her book, *Content Rules*, which she co-wrote with C.C. Chapman, sets the standard for creating new modes of optimized content for use in content marketing activities. Her second release, *Everybody Writes*, teaches people all over the globe how to create sticky content. Her books have been translated into many different languages and are used around the world as the benchmark for what makes online content worth reading.

Like many experts before her, Ann began her career as a journalist and an editor. She has been cited in *Forbes* as one of the most influential woman in social media, and she was also recognized by *Forbes Woman* as one of the top 20 women bloggers on the planet. Ann writes a column for *Entrepreneur* magazine and is a member of the LinkedIn Influencer program. She has also made it onto many lists as one of the most influential digital business leaders of our time.

Ann is so much more than just a great writer and a visionary in the digital content era. Her blog, AnnHandley.com, is one of the most entertaining methods by which one can learn about online content. She "practices what she preaches," which is her greatest strength as an expert.

Because Ann works so closely with content, she understands the relationship between SEO, content engagement, and the audience.

Her complete online profile is a testament to her in-depth understanding of these tools, and she is constantly helping MarketingProfs launch innovative content for a hungry marketing audience. We strongly advise you to follow her on social media, especially Twitter @annhandley.

---

38  Ann Handley Press, http://www.annhandley.com/press/

# WHY 99% OF NEW WEBSITES FAIL

*"Pretty websites . . . are rarely websites that convert as well as unpretty ones."*

Seth Godin, Best Selling Author

As active digital marketers, we have heard from an increasing number of business owners who feel shortchanged by the web design industry. Our industry has been selling them design-driven websites, when what they really need are optimized, revenue-generating inbound marketing platforms. When a new digital asset fails to generate sales, business owners feel they have been burned.

Design-driven "digital-brochure" websites are rarely engineered from the ground up to be SEO-friendly. This is the reason why 99% of new websites fail to achieve any meaningful, organic search engine visibility. In our industry, looks can be deceiving. Without SEO to glue the code, design, and content all together, a new website is destined for the search engine abyss.

## The Web Design Industry

One of the core reasons we decided to write this book was because of the endless stories we've heard from discouraged entrepreneurs. The story is always the same. They get a referral, hire a friend, or search online and select a web designer based on style and pricing.

Then, after the entire design and development process, the business owner discovers the site is not Google-friendly. Because of poor transitioning practices, previous SEO equity from the old site is lost or diminished. The new site launches and the business's rankings do not change at all, or worse yet, its rankings plummet and the phone stops ringing! Sure, the new website may look great, but a pretty little website buried in the depths of the cyber sea is a drowned investment.

QUICK TIP

While business owners expect to get a boost from the launch of a new website, most know very little about SEO or where their website should fit in the overall marketing puzzle. With the excitement of getting a new website created, search engine optimization is rarely discussed. Even if they did ask for "SEO"— a common marketing buzzword — most web design and development companies do not make SEO a major priority. In order to maximize your ROI on a new website, make SEO and the content of this book the foundation of any new web design project you undertake. When interviewing a new web design partner, make sure to discuss SEO, marketing goals, and ROI at length rather than only focusing on graphic design and website features.

We have heard grown men cry when told that their brand new website is virtually useless and that it may need a total redesign to achieve their SEO goals. Hearing this same story over and over again motivated us to do something about it. We became determined to write this book, get the word out, and inspire change.

We want to save the next business owner about to spend thousands of dollars on web design and development the agony of making one of the biggest mistakes in small-business marketing today. We also want the web design industry to embrace SEO and make it a fundamental part of all web development. Not all websites are created equal. Pretty does not mean practical! You don't buy a car because of its paint job, and you shouldn't buy a new website without discussing what's going under the hood.

## Web Design is Like Building a House

We call the above scenario "falling into the design trap." We sat down one day and asked ourselves why this travesty keeps happening over and over again in our industry. Then we realized — when business owners search for web design services, they are focusing on *design*. Most websites these days are, in fact, created by graphic designers.

A web design agency is typically chosen for its "style" or the look of its portfolio. The entrepreneur asks himself, "Does this company's design style match what I am looking for?" Then, when he believes he has found the right place, he engages its services. A proposal or project brief is presented that contains almost nothing about strategy or SEO. The website is built based on this design brief, which does not address any of the elements that Google needs to see or content that the company's ideal customers want to consume.

The problem is that website designers are digital artists. They are not marketing professionals or SEO consultants. And they are definitely not content marketers. In this sense, "website design" has become a victim of its own name. You need to realize that your *website* is no longer just a *site on the web*, and graphic design has become a digital commodity. Companies don't search for "inbound marketing platforms," but that is what your business needs to grow. Unfortunately, that's also not how the industry markets web design services. That needs to change.

If you have worked in digital marketing for any amount of time, you know that web designers often hold a disproportionate amount of influence over the web development process. Sometimes, a designer's whims and personal tastes can affect your corporate identity and messaging more that you realize. You will also find that many web designers learn just enough code so that they can launch websites on their own or in small teams. This means that the critical ingredients for online success — best-practices coding, search engine optimization, and marketing strategy — are rarely baked into new websites.

Allowing a web designer to drive the process means that you will receive a website built around personal tastes, rather than the business goals of your company. Therein lies the fundamental problem — the communication break-down — that causes so many business owners to spend a fortune on design before understanding the importance of websites in the modern era of marketing. [39]

Look at it this way: If a house were engineered and built by an interior designer, it would collapse. There is not a consumer in the world that would trust a designer to build her house. So how can it make sense to trust a designer to build a website that you expect to *perform* online?

It takes an entirely different set of skills to create an optimized inbound marketing platform, which is what you need to attract and convert traffic into sales. When you give a web designer the reigns, you miss out on an opportunity to create a high-performance website that functions as you need it to. [40] Instead of getting a Ferrari, you get a kit-car that looks good but has nothing under the hood.

---

39  7 Secrets Graphic Designers Won't Tell You About Effective Website Design, https://blog. kissmetrics.com/graphic-designer-secrets/

40  Phil Singleton, Boosting Conversions: 11 Experts Share Their Secrets, http://www. webdesignerdepot.com/2015/05/boosting-conversions-11-experts-share-their-secrets/

There are many good reasons why companies keep falling for these design-driven websites. Perhaps the main reason is due to all the low-cost web-builder websites that heavily advertise free or cheap *templated websites*. The reality is that most business owners have never even heard of inbound marketing. Some have heard of SEO, but it is little more than a buzzword to them. The end result is that business owners *price-shop* for design, when they should *results-shop* for performance.

In order to disrupt the status quo, web designers need to embrace marketing and SEO, and business owners need to recognize the importance of websites and treat them as true investments.

As an industry, we must pay more attention to content and SEO[41] during the design phase of website creation. We need to get marketing professionals, SEO experts, and content marketers in the room early. These critical elements must be taken into account from the very first line of code. Like it or not, business owners are starting to hold the web design industry accountable for search engine performance. Web designers need to understand that the end goal of creating a new website is to get the phone ringing, not just to deliver a spectacular piece of eye candy.

## The SEO-Content Balance

The world of website creation is split into two camps — the old way of designing for "good looks" and the new way of designing for *lead generation*. Websites exist to be found online, to attract visitors, and then to convert those visitors into paying customers. Looks matter, but not nearly as much as the marketing strategy behind your website.

There is too much competition online to be caught up in how flashy your website looks. Every day around the world, business owners are stepping into this bear trap, and it is a main reason why almost every new website fails to achieve search engine visibility. Your website needs

---

41   William Jones, How To Get Your High Google Rankings For Your Website in 2015, http://www.seoireland.net/how-to-get-high-google-rankings-for-your-website-in-2015/

to make a great first impression — that's a given — but it needs to deliver so much more.

We're in a battle for long-term, repeat customers. A great website not only sells well, but does so over and over again. That is why there has to be a shift from a focus on looks to what we call the "SEO-content balance." **Search engine strategy** pulls in the visitors, and content converts them. SEO is the dish that gets them in the door, and ongoing content is the cherry pie that keeps them coming back for more.

A design-driven process is perfect for print advertising and the classic "captive audience". But websites are very different. Your audience is not captive at all — they have total freedom of choice, and their choices are heavily influenced by Google. If viewers decide they don't like you, they're gone. And you'll struggle to get them back after that, especially if you failed to present your **unique selling proposition (USP)**.

The wording you use to sell customers in person or through outbound marketing may be very different from the type of content needed to

In order to create a powerful inbound marketing hub, you need to create a website around your ideal clients' search and content consumption habits. This is the only way to attract and close new clients through search engines. Strong SEO keyword research takes much of the guesswork out of web design by enabling you to reverse engineer a website around your ideal customers' search behavior, instead of relying on your best guess as to how they might be finding your products and services online.

attract the same type of customer to your online channels. Yet, because most businesses believe that "any existing copy or content will do," they place sales copy on their website, instead of developing the type of content that their ideal clients are searching for. Huge mistake.

Breakdowns can happen at any stage of this process. A website might have great SEO structure but contain terrible content. [42] When you succeed at getting lots of targeted visits but fail to convert, your inbound marketing strategy fails. Likewise, if the SEO is poor but the content is great, your website will never achieve its full revenue-generation potential. Lost at sea! For a website to truly take off, it must have a seamless SEO-content balance.

Search engine optimization takes care of the attraction element of your marketing strategy, while content takes care of customer conversion in the form of great web page copy, CTAs, and compelling blog posts.

## The Websites That Rank: Defined

Websites started out as simple pages but have evolved into web applications. Yet one powerful segment of the industry continues to market websites as digital brochures.

Companies mass-marketing cheap website solutions for free or for a "nominal" monthly fee are littered all over the website design industry. Sites like Wix, Weebly, SquareSpace, and GoDaddy are all culprits. They love to brainwash the market into believing that using their platform is all you need to succeed online, and it will only cost you $25 a month! Total hogwash. Let's be honest here: it is hard to find bad information about these website builders online, because they actively run content campaigns to promote positive sentiment about their services. Website builders are a nightmare for gaining SEO traction, proving the old adage "you get what you pay for."

---

42  Matt Southern, SEO and Content Marketing: How To Find The Perfect Balance Between Both, http://positionly.com/blog/seo/seo-content-marketing

The websites that genuinely rank well online are not made of generic code that has been duplicated 100,000 times. That is a fact. Website builders like these are less friendly to Google *crawlers*, and impossible to optimize to the extent of a custom website. [43] For competitive online niches, you need a custom website built with SEO in mind as it is developed.

Most of all, a website should be developed around the business's functional needs and underlying marketing goals, not shoe-horned into a template or pre-made theme. Pre-made *WordPress* themes, such as those sold on Themeforest, are not usually search engine-friendly. These themes look great and have many desirable features and functions, but ultimately they are designed to sell in volume. If you happen to know enough about technical SEO and coding, you can strip the junk code out of WordPress website templates and optimize them for search engines so that they rank just as well as a custom website. But it would take advanced knowledge to pull this off. When we use theme websites for our clients, we regularly give them extra attention, optimization, and tweaking.

These cheap-theme and website builder-sites condition business owners to think that low-cost solutions are viable, when they are not. You cannot have a website template or theme slapped up on a hosting account and expect it to start ranking on Google "out of the box." If that were the case, we'd all be using them.

**Your website is an investment, not an expense.** Business owners need to understand this distinction: to get a website to achieve and maintain organic rankings in a competitive niches, it takes more time, effort, and talent to build it right.

## Your Website's Ranking Potential

When it comes to SEO-friendly websites, there are no cheap solutions

---

43  Justin Harter, 21 Reasons Why You Shouldn't Use DIY Site Builders, http://superpixel. co/21-reasons-shouldnt-use-site-builder/

but plenty of snake oil. These days, your website is one of your company's most important assets. It's the first place people turn when they want information about your products or services, and the last place they check out before they make a purchasing decision. All of your sales, marketing, and advertising leads back to your website one way or another.

If you have a dated, unprofessional website, it tells your customer that you are a cheap, low-cost business. If you've seen it once, you've seen it a million times — that expensive print, television, or radio ad that drives people to the most awful, unprofessional website that is not optimized for sales conversions. Those clicks bounce right off the advertiser's site and onto competing sites that are doing it right.

Other business owners spend thousands of dollars on *pay-per-click ads* to compensate for their lack of SEO, but without the right content on their websites, their sales are still hanging off a cliff. Every week, we meet up with entrepreneurs who have invested tens of thousands of dollars in trade shows but are outraged when you suggest that their ten-year-old website needs an upgrade. Another great example is the business owner who invests tens of thousands into custom office, showroom, and conference room space, yet cringes at the idea of updating his website. Many more potential clients will visit your website before they ever consider stepping in your front door.

The sales cycle is broken at these companies, because the owners fail to acknowledge the Internet's role in modern purchasing decisions. If a website fails, a company's sales plan fails too.

The web design industry is broken, but that doesn't mean you have to buy another one of its empty-shell websites. Business owners who price-shop based on design quality often fail to see the bigger picture. Think of your website in terms of a key employment position. You don't hire candidates for a key position based on their looks and the lowest salary they will accept. You plan, interview, reference check, ask the right questions, and pay a competitive rate for the best talent.

**QUICK TIP** We have intentionally avoided using technical SEO language in this book and have instead focused on the assets, tools, and tactics that any business owner or web designer can use to drastically improve her organic search engine ranking potential. For an advanced, highly technical resource on search engine optimization, we highly recommend *The Art of SEO* by Eric Enge, Stephan Spencer, and Jessie C. Stricchiola. This 1,000-page textbook is a resource that every web designer and marketer should keep handy for reference.

Your website is a key asset, and it needs to be treated as an investment. It is not just another cost of doing business. By avoiding the pitfalls of the web design industry and investing in a professionally designed and optimized website, you will leapfrog past competitors stuck in the design trap.

## Expert to Watch: Eric Enge

Eric Enge has been an entrepreneur for thirty years and is one of the most influential people in SEO. Often cited as one of the world's top content marketing and SEO experts, his writing has helped shape the digital-marketing landscape for everyone online today.

Eric is the Founder and CEO of Stone Temple Consulting, which opened its doors in 1997. Eric began offering his customers SEO services in 2002 and quickly became a popular voice in the niche, publishing on top sites and becoming one of the Internet's most well-known personalities. Stone Temple Consulting helps other businesses improve their search engine visibility by taking a holistic approach to digital marketing.

On every Monday, Eric, together with Mark Traphagen, release a video on digital marketing topics called Here's Why. It is widely considered one of the best video broadcasts in the industry. Eric also speaks regularly at many of the large SEO conferences, including SMX, Pubcon, and ClickZ Live.

Eric regularly contributes to *Forbes*, Moz, Search Engine Land, and Copyblogger, and is a published author. In 2009 he released *The Art of SEO*, co-authored with other famous names in our niche like Stephan Spencer and Jessie Stricchiola. The 1000-page tome, now in its third edition, is considered to be the SEO Bible by many professionals.

Eric's articles on sites like *Forbes* and Search Engine Land are among the most technically accurate and often contain thought provoking predictions about the future of online marketing. He has a knack for predicting trends in the market, and was one of the first writers to foresee the end of content farms before the Panda update.

Eric is a key player in educating the industry about content marketing and its relationship to SEO. We strongly recommend that you sign up for his newsletter, "Eric Enge's Digital Marketing Newsletter," and follow him on Twitter, @stonetemple.

# THE STRATEGIC ADVANTAGE

*"It's much easier to double your business by doubling your conversion rate than by doubling your traffic."*

Jeffrey Eisenberg, Buyer Legends

The Wild-West era of simply launching a website on the Internet and staking your claim to first-page real estate ended a long time ago. The online space is crowded and more competitive than anyone wants to think about. A show-pony website would be great if outbound marketing still worked the way it used to, but we're in a world of inbound marketing now. You need to buckle up, cowboy, and get yourself a web-centric marketing system.

The search engines decide who gets to be found. Then the customer decides, based on your content, whether or not they will give you their business. You are not only judged by the search engine but also by the Internet at large. There is no way to grow in the new search engine economy without a top-notch strategy in place.

## A Website is not a Marketing Plan

Too many business owners still believe that a website makeover will solve their marketing problems, but a website is not a marketing plan. You can't just slap together a new website and expect that your business will thrive online by itself. The Internet has too many websites already — there are well over one billion online today. Leaving your defenseless website alone out there is akin to leaving a child alone on a busy New York street.

An overarching marketing plan, including an effective website, is essential for companies that want to remain competitive in their local or national markets. [44] There is an ever-growing number of consumers who buy online, but they have turned out to be the pickiest (and most educated) buyers of all time.

Purchasing decisions require influence, and influence requires digital strategy. The reality is that your product is going up against every other product just like yours. If you can't communicate your **unique selling proposition** and power it with an effective marketing strategy, you are in trouble.

Your website is the cornerstone of this digital strategy. It acts as your business headquarters in the virtual world. A successful website is not just an advertisement, it is part of the sales and marketing process. A website built without this in mind will shed conversions like cat hair.

In order for your website designer to create a website that is highly effective and accomplishes your marketing goals, you have to sit down and answer a long list of discovery questions. After all, you are creating your strategy first. This strategy will become the basis for your marketing plan, and it is what will fuel new sales growth through your website.

---

44  A Website Is Not Enough: How To Build an Online Marketing Strategy and Measure Results, http://wordpress.tv/2013/12/04/a-web-site-is-not-enough-how-to-build-an-online-marketing-strategy-and-measure-results/

You will have to answer questions such as:

- Who, *exactly*, is your ideal target audience?
- What type of content does your target audience like to consume?
- What are the goals that you hope to accomplish with your website and marketing?
- Which search terms does your target audience use when they need your product or service?

These questions are just a few mild instigators to get your creative juices going. You absolutely have to answer them so that you know *exactly* who you are building your website for. If you don't, your web designer will build a site based on his personal taste rather than a sound marketing strategy. You can't really expect a web designer to know your customers or business like you do.

## Strategy Comes Before Tactics

Anyone can launch a ship into the cyber sea. But without setting a course, that ship will drift aimlessly until it dashes itself on the rocks and sinks. Your website is your digital headquarters, and it should be engineered to funnel and convert prospects using the best marketing tactics for your business.

A strategy comprises the top-level goals for your business, while tactics are the lower-level actions or steps taken to achieve these goals. An overall marketing plan could consist of several strategies and hundreds of tactics. Each platform can have a strategy that feeds into your main marketing plan. This main plan is sometimes called your *digital marketing strategy*, which encompasses all sales strategies that you execute online. Your website is a pillar of your entire marketing strategy.

Before you have even considered the aesthetics of your website, you need to define your marketing strategy. Strategy always comes first. Once you have committed to a strategy and have developed a tactical plan to achieve your strategic goals, you are in an ideal position to create the perfect website.

**QUICK TIP** Your website strategy may have a few major top-tier goals, including rankings, sales, conversion rates or traffic generation stats. The tactics you use to achieve these goals on your website may include email marketing, website copy optimization, promotions, Facebook and Twitter marketing, and landing page creation. Together these tactics add up to your website strategy.

Without strategy, your tactics are random because they do not add up to any top-tier goals. [45] You cannot accurately measure success without clearly defined goals. But if you think about it, many businesses create websites impulsively and then roll the dice with various marketing tactics. Tactics before strategy rarely work, but strategy before tactics almost always does.

A website has a specific set of needs that must be fulfilled in order for it to be successful. It is up to each business to set the right goals. They usually involve a strong purpose and a clear vision. Most businesses have annual financial goals for their websites; they can also include a number of key metrics that analysts use to measure the rate of online sales.

How do you create a marketing strategy?

Start by asking yourself:

- Why you do what you do?
- Who you do it for?
- What do you do that makes your company remarkable and unique?

---

45 Jeremiah Owyang, The Difference Between Strategy and Tactics, http://www.web-strategist.com/blog/2013/01/14/the-difference-between-strategy-and-tactics/

## Determining Your Strategic Purpose

Knowing how to create a strategy like a certified marketing pro may require specialized training and years of practical experience, but the basics remain the same. You can determine your company's strategic purpose online on your own. Putting some thought into strategy prior to engaging a web designer or starting new website development will dramatically improve the project's return on investment.

### *Set a clear purpose and mission (Why?)*

By outlining your purpose and mission, you can get to your bottom line, which means greater levels of business satisfaction. You might relish the fact that your service delivers products faster than anyone else. Or that it fulfills a client's need in an original way. Every business has one defining purpose, the decision-driver that helps you define your brand. What is yours? Spend a few minutes answering this one question, and it will be the starting point for a powerful and successful strategy that will take your business exactly where you want it to go.

There is a reason why digital marketers create detailed buyer personas; the more you understand your key target demographic — what they look like, how they behave, what they think about, their likes and dislikes — the better your marketing content will be. This all adds up to a website that performs better for these individuals, the ones that love giving you money.

*Determine your ideal target demographic (Who?)*

You need to understand who it is you are trying to help. Business is about problem-solving and understanding your ideal customer is the key. Without knowledge on your "who," you will not be able to build a viable strategy. Not everyone will care why you are doing what you do, but there will be people that value it. These are your "business drivers."

When you target your business drivers, you get to know the customers that bring you the majority of your sales, the ones that advocate for your business. By investing in them and building your website around how they behave and what they want, you will attract the highest quality prospects. Develop a highly detailed ideal customer profile and use it.

*Define your unique selling proposition (What sets you apart?)*

Finally, you need to understand what your business does that is remarkable and different in your market.[46] What makes you special among your competitors? This goes beyond knowing your niche, it is about standing apart from others that claim to be able to achieve what you can.

Consumers expect a fair price, good service, and a bold selection. These are expectations, not differentiators. You need to exceed consumer expectations if you are going to make an impact. How you choose to treat them, how you make them feel, and how you behave in your business can all be part of your USP.

## Identifying Your Ideal Client

Perhaps the most important of these aspects is the identification of your ideal target customer. You cannot create a strong marketing strategy without this knowledge. To know thy business, you must know thy customer. That way, the development of your message, service, product,

---

46  Dan Shewan, How To Create a Ferocious Unique Selling Proposition, http://www.wordstream.com/blog/ws/2014/04/07/unique-selling-proposition

sales, and support will hit the mark with your buying public every time.

You cannot be everything to everyone, and trying to be that way makes you nothing instead. That is why investing time and real effort into the intimate discovery of your ideal customer is totally worth it. First things first: how do you discover who they are?

Find a highly targeted group of people that believe your USP. This group must be narrow in the sense that it has a very specific need or problem. Pick the smallest possible market, one to whom you can deliver solutions that will transform buyers into brand advocates or raving fans of your company. You can always redefine and expand to a larger market later on.

Once you have done this, you must create your initial value hypothesis; in other words, you need to answer the question why your ideal client should use your company. This will become the main reason your company is special and attracts your target demographic. This is why your customers choose you over competitors.

Discovery and testing are your next steps. You must develop your customer theory and then test it in the open market. Without customer interaction, you need to get creative. New businesses often have few or no prospects with whom to interact. If that is your situation, you may have to think outside the box.

The needs of your ideal target demographic are constantly changing, so do not forget to update this information every few months, or implement a system whereby feedback is part of your marketing cycle. Once you have tested the marketing, you can "sketch" your ideal customer. This is the discovery and defining stage of buyer persona creation. [47]

Gather all of the insight and tiny details that you need to paint a picture of your ideal customer group. Social media makes this process

---

47  Pamela Vaughan, How To Create Detailed Buyer Personas For Your Business [Free Persona Template], http://blog.hubspot.com/blog/tabid/6307/bid/33491/Everything-Marketers-Need-to-Research-Create-Detailed-Buyer-Personas-Template.aspx

Do some test-marketing to reach out to your identified target demographic. Collect feedback on your company, products, and services. Heck, offer free samples in return! Your ultimate goal is to engage these "ideals"; to figure out how they think, what they want, what does not work, and how you can best service their needs

a lot easier. You can discover how people behave simply by monitoring their social responses to content much of the time. Build a full, color picture of these people or create several custom profiles, depending on your research.

You will use this vital information to formulate your marketing strategy so that you can explode onto the online scene and grow at a faster rate than most other companies.

## The Marketing Hourglass: Plan Development

You have probably heard of a marketing or sales funnel, right? Leads are poured into the top of a large opening and funneled through a system of "tactics" until customers come out the bottom at the final destination, usually your website. This is an old marketing practice that has become incredibly outdated for one vital reason —the chase.

In this new age of modern marketing, chasing customers is out, and developing long-term relationships with repeat customers is in. This model does not fit with the old sales funnel concept, which is why the marketing hourglass was created. It uses the same open attraction of the funnel concept, while continuing through to the end-*user experience*, leading to repeat sales.

Leads are actively converted into customers that will not only just pay, but are attached to the brand and will return again and again. This increases the chance of repeat sales over time and lifelong loyalty to the business involved. There are seven phases of this marketing hourglass.

**Know > Like > Trust > Try > Buy > Repeat > Refer**

As you may have realized by this self-explanatory phase process, the end goal is to get the customer to refer you to more customers, converting them into a brand advocate. This will help your business grow organically online.

Loads of companies get stuck creating their marketing plan.[48] It can be tough bringing one to life, especially when you are not familiar with the moving parts. You can end up with a Frankenstein of a plan, and it might not even be good enough to use. We suggest you consult a certified marketing expert for this, but you can also work on one yourself which will help them when the time comes.

- First, look at who matters most in your business. A good marketing plan is based on serving a niche market well. Be specific, build your buyer personas, and focus on being the best for those people.

- Second, look at your competitors. How are they likely to respond to your offering? Focus on their USPs, any advantages they have, and how you might overcome them. The formula becomes: know thy business, know thy customers and thy competitors. You are up against these companies; you better come out swinging.

- Next, set your business apart based on this customer and competitor data. You need to be different to stand out. Different is always better. Do not pitch your product or service like your competitors do, or you will lose business. Focus on customer frustrations and needs; solve their core problems. Figure out what your brand symbolizes and declare it to the world.

---

48  Andrew Klausner, Creating a Successful Marketing Strategy, http://www.forbes.com/sites/advisor/2013/04/17/creating-a-successful-marketing-strategy/

- After that, turn to your nuts and bolts. An effective marketing plan incorporates multiple channels, including social media, email, and mobile marketing. These are all critical to SEO and the content-conversion balance that you need to create.

Once your strategy is in place and your tactics have been outlined, you are almost done. The last thing you need to do is determine how much time and money you will spend on each tactic, working back until you get to your website. Create an action list and get to work.

## Bake Your Marketing Plan Into Your Website

Remember that delicious cherry pie, baked just for your ideal customer? That is what your website should be like. When we say bake your marketing plan into your website, we mean you need to integrate all of your marketing tactics into your site so that it delivers what your customer really wants. You promised that pie, and by all things holy, you will deliver it!

Your website needs to tell your story in a way that differentiates you from your competitors. It should contain valuable, relevant information that your ideal customer needs. Engaging content is sticky and will keep them coming back. Your website should also make your USP very clear, leaving no room for doubt or confusion.

Your strategy needs to be woven into the DNA of your website, from top to bottom. Contrary to popular belief, it's not the design that makes customers come back, it's the content. Content is the sweet icing and sprinkles that everyone wants. Blogs, social media posts on Facebook and Twitter, Reddit posts, and Google+ can all add to your unique brand identity, based on your website strategy.

Your site should also be easy to enjoy. It has to be ultra-simple for your ideal customer to navigate and use on all fronts. Include trustworthy information that will make the purchase-decision journey a quick one. Your website should quickly answer all questions that your ideal customer has about your product or service.

Bake mobile usability into your website as well. [49] In fact, consider designing for the mobile user first! The people that visit your online store show up from multiple places, and data has shown that mobile phones and tablets are getting more and more of the action. Meet their needs, or they will click over to website of a competitor who cared enough to make it truly mobile-friendly.

The website experience should be pleasant and memorable, with all the built-in functionality needed to rise in the oven and be more delicious than your burnt competitors. Websites should be quick to load and have ready-to-go email campaigns and sticky content that keeps *bounce rates* nice and low.

At the end of this extensive process (not quick, easy, or cheap), your website will be the culmination of all the time, energy, and effort that you have put into identifying your customer, defining her needs, perfecting your USP, and developing your marketing plan. You cannot put the "cart before the horse," as they say.

Step one is your marketing plan. Step two is your website. Not the other way around. It is about time someone started to shout this from the mountain tops so that small business owners stop wasting their time and money. Your website will never reach its full ranking or ROI potential without a marketing plan. That is the ultimate truth.

## *Expert to Watch: Brian Halligan*

Brian Halligan is the Co-founder and CEO of HubSpot. Prior to HubSpot, Brian was a venture partner at Longworth Ventures and VP of Sales at Groove Networks, which was acquired by Microsoft. Previously, Brian was a Senior VP at PTC.

Brian has co-authored two books: *Inbound Marketing: Get Found Using Google, Social Media, and Blogs* with co-founder Dharmesh Shah; and *Marketing Lessons from the Grateful Dead* with David Meerman Scott and Bill Walton.

---

49  Sergio Aicardi, 7 Key Pieces of Advice About Web Content Strategy From Matt Cutts, http://contentmarketinginstitute.com/2015/01/advice-web-content-strategy-matt-cutts/

Brian currently teaches a business class at MIT Sloan, called Designing, Developing and Launching Successful Products in an Entrepreneurial Environment. Brian serves on the Board of Directors for Fleetmatics Group, a global provider of fleet management systems.

He was named Ernst and Young's Entrepreneur of the Year in 2011, a Glassdoor 25 Highest Rated CEO in 2014 and 2015, and an Inc. Founders 40 in 2016. Around the community, Brian works with Camp Harbor View, a special camp for at-risk youth in Boston, which serves approximately one thousand kids each summer.

HubSpot was founded in 2006, when Brian Halligan and co-founder Dharmesh Shah came to the realization that the way people shop and buy had dramatically changed. While customers could now research independently over the internet and on social media, most businesses still relied on outdated marketing and sales tactics like cold calling and direct mailing.

In response, the co-founders created a new, "inbound" way of marketing and selling, leveraging new tools like blogging, email, social media, landing pages, and forms, to reach customers in a more helpful and human way.

Now, more than ten years later, HubSpot is the world's leading inbound marketing and sales platform. Over 19,000 customers in more than 90 countries use HubSpot's software, services, and support to transform the way they attract, engage, and delight customers.

# 07

# IT ALL STARTS WITH KEYWORDS

*"[Content Marketing is] a more competitive environment certainly, but those who have real empathy for web users and influencers AND have the SEO skills to infuse their work with great keyword targeting, search accessibility, etc., are going to have ongoing success."*

Rand Fishkin, Moz

This may be the most important chapter in this book, so pay attention. This is the time to perk up, regain focus, and buckle down. If there is such a thing as SEO secret sauce, this may be it. It is well-known that SEO experts never give all of their best secrets away. Why would they?

In this chapter, we aim to change that. Because it all starts with keywords. Everything. Google's entire algorithm is based around them. When you know how to conduct accurate keyword research and apply it to the right marketing strategy, magic can happen. Likewise, if you target or prioritize the wrong keywords, your SEO campaign will never reach its potential.

## The Keyword Conundrum

In order for your SEO strategy to succeed, particularly at the tactical level, you need solid keyword research from the very beginning. Your keyword research, and the master list that you develop from this intensive research, will become the foundation of your on-page SEO, off-page SEO, and content marketing strategies.

Executing an inbound marketing strategy without knowledge of your ideal customers' search habits is akin to running a race in which you have not located the finish line. Believe us when we say that this is the key step to calibrating your content strategy with your ranking goals, and the key component for every successful SEO strategy.

With search engines, everything boils down to words and phrases. It does not matter what type of content you are searching for, every Internet search is related to a string of words or even a single one. Your website is home to many words. They exist in the title and text of your blog posts, on web pages, and in your downloadable site files.

They can also be found in your browser titles and meta-descriptions, even though these are not visible on your front-end web pages.

**Page Title:** All web pages have their own browser titles. The page title is part of a web page's HTML code and appears in the title bar of your web browser. Page titles are displayed in the search results, most often as the blue linked text.

**Meta Description:** Also called a page description, a meta description is a short description of the content on any given web page. It is laid out in HTML code and does not appear on the website. It is, however, displayed in the search engine results under the blue linked text.

Words also appear in the main website address and the URL of your web pages and blog posts. Words can be tied to images, audio, and video content on your website, along with structured data. **Structured data** is special website code that gives the search engines extra information about the content on your website; that information is sometimes displayed in search results, such as star ratings.

Search engines try to make sense of the words on your site, along with words on other websites that are associated with yours, and how users engage with your content. Google wants you to create pages for users, not for search engines. This is an SEO law. Yet most people only want to rank on the search engines in order to get the phone to ring; they could care less about engagement.

Many people still see blogging and social media as a chore. But to get your ideal customers through Google, you have to know how to create a path of high-quality content. This is not just about organic SEO — all inbound marketing strategies require a consistent and variable flow of high-quality content. Ironically, great content will not achieve its ranking goals unless it has an underlying keyword strategy behind it.

## Preparing a Keyword Strategy

Google makes the lion's share of its revenue from AdWords. The AdWords platform is only successful because the vast majority of Internet users rely on Google Search to access information and to find the best products and services.

Google wants to provide you with as much information as possible, so that you can create PPC ads that will siphon clicks away from the **organic search results**. That is why Google sets extremely high standards on AdWords ad copy and offers you information and tools to help you improve elements of your campaign, like **click-through rates** and quality scores.

Take a moment to think about that . . .

Google wants to *help* you to create an AdWords ad so compelling, it will actively persuade an Internet user to choose the paid ad over one of its organic search results. When you understand how important AdWords is to Google, then you begin to understand why AdWords is also very important for organic search engine optimization.

We believe that AdWords provides the astute SEO professional with a window into the Google algorithm. [50] We take nothing for granted in how it is set up, what information AdWords provides, and the many tools Google provides to help us create effective PPC ads.

Once you have a core list of keywords, there are a number of tools that will help you build a larger list. There are also processes that will help you refine and prioritize your keywords. Before you start building that list, you need to understand where your business is today, and where you want it to go.

## ASK YOURSELF OR YOUR CLIENT THESE TEN SEO DISCOVERY QUESTIONS:

**1. What does your revenue pie chart look like today?**
Reviewing the revenue breakdown is one way to get your head around a business, especially if you are a web designer trying to build an SEO-friendly website for a client.

---

50 Stephen Kapusta, Target AdWords Competitor Keywords The Right Way, http://www.lunametrics.com/blog/2015/05/13/target-adwords-competitor-keywords-rlsa/

**2. What would you like your revenue pie chart to look like in the future?**
Your current stream of revenues may not be the ideal stream. If 80% of your revenue comes from lower-margin products or services, you may want to develop an SEO strategy around that other 20%.

**3. What are the 5-10 root keywords that are most relevant to your business?**
Your guess at your ideal customers' search habits could end up being quite different from the way they actually search. Writing down an initial list of your "guesstimates," however, is a good place to start.

**4. Which of your competitors have strong search engine visibility today?**
Take a close look at your competitors' websites. You are now six chapters into this book — we guarantee that you are not looking at websites or rankings the way you were before.

**5. What industries or vertical markets do your customers come from?**
Take a step back and consider your ideal customers from multiple perspectives; it will help you engineer high-quality content with the right keyword choices.

**6. What are the interests and demographics of your ideal customer?**
The more you understand about your target customer, the stronger you can make your website content to draw them in and convert them.

**7. How do your customers define your products and services?**

Think about how your customers understand your products and services, their uses, and the problems they solve.

**8. Where are your ideal customers located?**

You must know where your ideal customers are located so that you can understand what cities your prospective customers are searching for [city] + [root keyword], like "Kansas City marketing consultants."

**9. What time of year do your ideal customers buy products and services?**

Understanding key purchasing cycles can give you insight into the right word choices for your ongoing SEO efforts and how to work these into your content marketing plan.

**10. How do your ideal clients buy products in your segment?**

Take into consideration how your customers buy, and it will help you optimize your content and develop high converting CTAs.

*Now write down your list of 5-10 core keywords based on your answers above:*

_____

_____

_____

_____

# How to Perform SEO Keyword Research

Our secret weapon for keyword research is the Google AdWords Keyword Planner. AdWords is Google's advertising system. The Keyword Planner is a free tool in AdWords that gives you fantastic information for building and refining a highly targeted keyword list.

The catch? As of 2016, you may need an active AdWords account to use the Keyword Planner, and Google is starting to show signs limiting this tool's usage.

Google offers you some great tips on how to best use its Keyword Planner tool for AdWords.[51] This knowledge, combined with what we are about to show you, will help you generate a list of keywords to use as the foundation of your SEO and content marketing strategy.

### *Generate a Raw Keyword List*

- **Step 1:** Sign-up for Google AdWords here: **https://www.google.com/adwords/**

- **Step 2:** Access the Keyword Planner in your AdWords account. *AdWords > Top Menu Bar > Tools & Analysis > Keyword Planner*

- **Step 3:** Click on the selection for "Search for new keywords using a phrase, website, or category."

- **Step 4:** In that same section, navigate to "Targeting" and select the geographic area that you want to target. You can select a country, state, metro area, or zip code, including multiple locations and variations of locations.

- **Step 5:** You should already have a raw list of at least 5-10 root keywords for an initial search. Type in these words or copy them into the first box. We like to leave all other fields blank on the initial search, and leave other options in their default positions.

---

51 Using Keyword Planner To Get Keyword Ideas and Traffic Forecasts, https://support.google.com/adwords/answer/2999770?hl=en

This includes the default data range that covers Google's search data for the last 12 months. Next, click the "get ideas" button, and a keyword report will be generated.

- **Step 6:** In this report, you will find all the pre-determined AdWords Ad Groups that Google deems relevant or related to your root keywords. The report shows a bar graph of search volumes, which gives you an indication of seasonality and related peaks and valleys in search activity over the last twelve months. Focus on these:

  - ➢ **Ad Groups:** Google automatically creates keyword groups. This can give you insight as to how Google associates keywords with one another and some clues for determining keyword relevance.

  - ➢ **Avg. Monthly Searches:** The average number of times people have searched for this exact keyword based on the date range and targeting settings that you have selected. If Google does not have enough data, a dash (–) will appear.

  - ➢ **Competition:** The level of bidding competition for a given keyword. Google calculates the number of advertisers bidding on each keyword relative to all keywords across Google Search. A lack of data is represented by the dash (–).

  - ➢ **Suggested Bid:** This is Google's suggested bid for a given keyword. It is calculated by taking into account the ***cost-per-click (CPC)*** that advertisers are paying for this keyword, based on the location and search network setting you have selected. The amount is an estimate, and Google warns that your actual ***CPC*** may vary somewhat.

  - ➢ **Ad Impression Share:** *AdWords impression share* is the number of impressions you have received divided by the total number of searches for the location and network you are targeting that exactly matched your keyword in the last month. This metric helps you identify potential opportunities that your keyword has to get impressions and clicks.

- **Step 7:** Scroll through this list of ad groups and take note of the averages. Click down into each group to view the monthly averages for individual keywords and phrases.

- **Step 8:** Start building a spreadsheet by clicking on the "Add to Plan" double arrow link (>>). When you click the (>>) button, it will select your keyword ad groups, which you can then use to build an excel spreadsheet of keywords.

- **Step 9:** Once you have successfully selected all of the Ad Groups you would like to include in your keyword list, you can download them in a single .csv file from the right side of the page. This can be easily be saved or converted into a Microsoft Excel file. [52]

**QUICK TIP** Do not only look for keywords that have the most searches. The idea is to identify the keywords that have a combination of high volume, higher suggested starting bids, and higher competition value. These are your "money words". If your competitors are bidding higher click prices for specific terms, it says that those are the ones converting into sales better than other terms.

---

52 Google AdWords Keyword Tools Is a Beginner Keyword Research Tool, http://www. wordstream.com/adwords-keyword-tool

## Clean and Process Your Keyword List

Once you have downloaded your raw list of keywords, you need to go through each keyword phrase line by line. Depending on the size of your initial list, you could be doing this with hundreds of keywords. As you scroll through them, begin to delete words that are not related to, or would not be a target for, your business.

Take note that the list of keywords, as well as their grouping and ordering, is not random. The Keyword Planner algorithmically determined that those words are directly or indirectly related to your group of targeted keywords. As you delete and prioritize your keyword list, ask yourself these important questions:

➤ What keywords should I target for my home page?

➤ What keywords should I target for my core inner pages and other subpages?

➤ What new pages can I create, or how can I restructure my website based on this new, relevant keyword data?

➤ How can I use this data to create a content calendar for my content marketing goals and blog posts?

➤ How can I use this data to identify strategic partners or guest-blogging targets on third party websites?

➤ Is there information in this data that helps me identify any niches that I can use for online and offline marketing?

### Develop a Shorter List

You now have your list of keywords from Google, but that does not mean that you have the keys to your SEO kingdom just yet. Keyword Planner helps you look at keywords from the inside out. Now you need to look at them from the outside in. It is time for the spot test.

Spend some time spot testing some "money words" from your list:

• Run an organic search on Google's homepage. Pay close attention to your auto-fill results. Google wants to steer your search to high-converting keywords that are relevant to what it thinks you are searching for.

- Look at the ad copy in the AdWords ads for your test searches. Look for patterns and repeating keywords that show up in other PPC ads on the results page.
- Look at the organic results on those same pages. Check the blue titles in the results and pay close attention to the words and word positioning.
- Look at competitor websites that are beating yours for your most coveted keywords. Notice their page titles and web copy. See if there are other words or phrase variations to add to your own list.
- If you have access to premium tools or services like SEMRush.com and Ahrefs.com, gather organic and PPC keyword data on your competitor websites for use in your SEO strategy.
- Now that you have completed the keyword generation and refinement process, you have a stronger list of keywords. Run these through the Keyword Planner again to see if any new keyword opportunities or ad groups appear. Repeat the process if necessary.

## The Content-Driven SEO Strategy

Now you can see why we devoted all of the previous chapter to marketing strategy, and why marketing professionals have an inherent edge when it comes to content-driven SEO. To develop the best possible keyword list for SEO, you have to get your head around the business first.

That means deep exploration into your marketing goals, how your ideal customers consume content, and how they search for information, products, and services on the Internet.

If you have developed a marketing strategy, you will be in a better position to develop a keyword list, genetically engineer SEO-friendly websites, and execute perfect content-driven SEO strategies. You know who your ideal customers are, what kind of content, they want, and what keywords they use.[53] The roadmap to success is coming together.

There are some excellent tools that will help you identify the kind of content that is trending and what topics are hot at the moment. With this information, you can attempt to create the kind of content that people will want right now, while baking in your marketing and keyword goals. This is how you create a recipe for targeted, strategic SEO-friendly content.

BuzzSumo, for example, is a great tool for content discovery. It shows you what is getting the most engagement *right now*, in real time. You do not want to copy what other people are doing, but this data gives you insight on what type of content your niche finds most interesting and is attracting the greatest number of social signals and sharing.

Just as Keyword Planner helps take the guesswork out of keyword research, BuzzSumo helps take the guesswork out of creating new content with high-engagement potential. Peanut butter and chocolate.

With your marketing strategy and plan in place, a highly targeted list of keywords and a content calendar, the time has come to begin creating content for your ideal customers.

**QUICK TIP** Create a content calendar with the end goal of creating an eBook. Think of 10-15 titles on a table of contents that will work as standalone blog posts. At the end of the blog series, stitch these blog posts into an eBook, and use it as a call to action carrot to grow the email list in your website.

---

53  Garrett Moon, An SEO Driven Approach To Content Marketing: The Complete Guide, http://coschedule.com/blog/content-marketing-seo/

*Choose from:*

- ✓ Web page copy
- ✓ Blog posts
- ✓ Guest blog posts
- ✓ Sponsored posts on authority sites
- ✓ Landing Pages
- ✓ Press releases
- ✓ Web videos

- ✓ Podcasts
- ✓ Slideshare presentations
- ✓ Social media posts (like on LinkedIn Pulse)
- ✓ Infographics
- ✓ Webinars
- ✓ eBooks
- ✓ Whitepapers

As you can see in the graphic above, our approach to SEO combines marketing strategy, keyword analysis, and content creation. This is how you build a powerful SEO campaign.

## Keywords in Content: The Difference

You have learned how to identify keywords, how to use those keywords to create new content, and what type of content you should be creating for your ideal customers. Your priority should be creating interesting and engaging content for your audience.

Keywords cannot drive the content creation process, but you should actively try and work targeted keywords into your content in a natural way that does not detract from its quality. In other words, don't create content just for SEO, but never create any new content without your SEO goals in mind.

➢ **Home Page**: Generally speaking, this page carries more inherent ranking potential than any of your inner pages. Many SEO experts focus their main keyword or keywords here. For most websites, it is helpful to have 200-300 words of static (i.e. permanent) intro text, including your main keyword(s) and a few variations thereof.

➢ **Core Inner Pages**: For small business websites, there should be at least 3-5 core inner pages to describe business segments or product lines in detail. These are the pages where we focus on important, other high-priority keyword themes, page by page. While there is no set rule for word count, in general, pages with at least 500 words or more tend to perform better than those with just a few sentences.

➢ **Supplemental Inner Pages**: You will also optimize other important pages on your website, such as your Contact, About Us, and FAQ pages.

➢ **Blog Pages:** Individual blog posts are critical for inbound marketing on many levels, especially for on-page and off-page SEO. Blog posts are one of the best methods for targeting *long-tail keywords*, and geo-targeting locations. There is no set rule for word count, although many SEOs suggest a 500-word minimum. The industry trend is to create longer, more in-depth blog posts of 1,000 to 2,500 words or more, as longer blog posts seem to be getting more traction.

As you create website pages, your page titles and blog post titles, and any other content to be posted on your site, social media channels, or third party websites, always consider keyword opportunities.[54]

Pay close attention to **long-tail keyword phrases** that relate to how Internet users are searching for information, as opposed to those on the purchase path. As you process and analyze your keyword list, you should think about how you can weave search patterns into a content calendar.

New blog posts, for example, would warrant this line of questioning:

- ✓ On which keyword can I focus for this post?
- ✓ How can I create an interesting title for this post that has the root keyword or a variation of my targeted keyword?
- ✓ How can I write this post with SEO in mind while keeping my readers' best interests first?
- ✓ How should I customize the link for my post so that the targeted keyword is included in the link structure?
- ✓ Can I link to any authority sites in this post in a way that adds editorial value?
- ✓ What rich media (embedded video, tweets, images) can I include in this post that would add value?
- ✓ Can I tag any media, like an image, with the targeted keyword?
- ✓ What section subtitles can I create that add value to post?

---

54  David Reich, Where and When Your Keywords Really Matter For Content Marketing & SEO, http://contentmarketinginstitute.com/2011/10/keywords-for-content-marketing-and-seo/

> ✓ Can I use this post as an opportunity to target another geographic territory in a way that makes sense and adds value to the post?
>
> ✓ Where can I link to other posts and pages on my website that will fit in naturally with the content and add value to the post?

Keyword research will give you a goldmine of inspiration to create dynamic web content and blog posts that your ideal customers are searching for every day. It also sheds light on the new business and strategic partnership opportunities available to you.

**This is the heart and soul of modern SEO: reverse engineering content around search behavior.** Keyword research not only tells you where the fish are biting, but what they are biting on.

## Expert to Watch: Larry Kim

Who better to follow in the field of keyword research than Larry Kim, founder and Chief Technology Officer of WordStream, Inc.,[55] one of the world's most successful digital marketing firms.

Larry started WordStream in 2007 while providing Internet marketing services to clients. At the same time, he managed a team of engineers and marketers developing and selling software for *search engine marketing automation*.

Larry has also written four award-winning books on software development and blogs regularly for WordStream, Search Engine Journal, Marketing Profs, *Forbes*, Search Engine Land, Search Engine Watch, HubSpot, Moz, and Social Media Today. His content generates around 2 million pageviews *per month*.

---

55  Larry Kim, Founder and Chief Technology Officer, http://www.wordstream.com/larry-kim

Voted the most influential PPC expert in 2013 and 2014, Larry regularly wins business awards for his contributions to SEO and PPC advertising. He speaks at conferences all over the world and is one of the most prominent search engine thought leaders today. We highly recommend reading the WordStream blog and following him on Twitter @larrykim.

# 08

# BUILDING STRONGER WEBSITE SEO

*"When a designer gives you a bill, what do you see it as? An expense, right? When a designer gives me a bill, I see it as an investment. For me, it is something that appreciates and helps your business grow."*

Neil Patel, Crazy Egg

In this new age of content-driven SEO, you need to strike a balance between search engine optimization and design. SEO leads the horses to water, **user experience**, design, and content get them to drink.

Modern web design is not about winning an imaginary design competition. It's about winning the marketing war. To win this war, the balance must be clear and functional, built not only to impress but also to convert. This chapter delves into the mechanics of building an SEO-friendly website.

## SEO and Design: The Balance

Don't get the wrong idea about search engine optimization professionals. We don't hate pretty websites; far from it. But few outside of our discipline understand the devastation that a one-track focus can have on a business website. Designing a website for looks alone will result in a weak website that does not generate new sales.

Creativity and flow are more important to the average web designer than SEO and *lead generation*. [56] Yet, when an SEO company has to come in and fix a website after the fact, it usually takes a lot more time and effort than building it right from the ground up.

As we've emphasized, search engine optimization is just as important, if not more important, than design. Websites need to attract visitors, keep them on the website, and convert them into sales. Design is a part of the process, but should not dominate it.

This problem still exists in the web development world because designers do not want search engines to dictate or influence design. As web designers, we have to change this mindset.

How bad can it get? Consider the commercial airline Ryan Air. Ryan Air redesigned its website in 2014, ignoring SEO in the process, which resulted in a devastating blow to its rankings.[57] Its previously strong Google rankings tanked during the busiest time of the year. This kind of redesign ranking nightmare happens to tens of thousands of businesses every year.

## Treat Your Website as an Investment

As an entrepreneur, the onus is on you. Business owners must view websites as an investment and not an expense or a cost of doing business. Rather than price-shopping web-design services, website solutions need to be procured and maintained like any other revenue generating asset. Business owners need to emphasize both SEO and design to get a

---

56  Dorian Travers, Web Design Vs SEO Finding The Balance, http://www.mycustomer.com/blogs-post/web-design-vs-seo-finding-balance/164971

57  Gwyn Topham. Ryanair drops out of top Google flight search results after website overhaul. http://www.theguardian.com/business/2014/apr/17/ryanair-website-drops-out-top-google-flight-search-results

modern, functional website. And they need to do it by working with a company that honors both.

If you are looking for new web designer or for help identifying web development companies that understand inbound marketing and search engine optimization, consider reading the eBook **How to Hire A Web Designer: And Not Get Burned By Another Agency**. It includes questions to ask, red flags to avoid, what you should pay for a new website, and everything you need to look at "under the hood" of a web design agency. Request a free PDF copy here:

**http://kcwebdesigner.com/how-to-hire-a-web-designer/**

Responsibility also lies with web design firms. If you are a web designer, discussing the project's ROI should be priority number one. Don't brush off SEO, as it will come back to haunt you.

Unfortunately, there are still many digital agencies that operate according to their own self-interest, even if it goes against the best interests of their clients. They have always built design-driven websites, and they have to keep business rolling in. Change is the most difficult for these kinds of agencies.

At the end of the day, businesses need websites that give Google what it needs to rank them and ideal customers what they want to see to choose them. Managing this balance is the key to web design. Web designers and SEO pros need to come together to create truly SEO-friendly websites.

## Performing a Website Analysis

Before any decisions can be made about your SEO strategy or even considering a website redesign, you may want to think about getting a professional audit of your current one.

If you partner with an SEO company for this, it will want to conduct a website analysis to gauge its current SEO value. [58] On-page elements account for roughly half of a website's ranking potential. Website audits can be detailed and comprehensive. They will tell you how and where to fix your website's SEO issues.

An SEO audit will also help you identify the existing SEO equity of your site, so that you can mitigate the risk of losing rankings when transitioning to a new website. A website SEO analysis will also help you understand what you need to do to improve your ranking potential.

---

**HOW YOU CAN RUN A BASIC SEO SITE AUDIT:**

- Run a report on your website. We offer a free SEO website reporting tool that covers many of the basics: **https://seoforgrowth.com/website-seo-checker**

- Review your website in Google Search Console and Google Analytics. These free tools can tell you a lot about the SEO-health of your website.

- Review your findings with your web developer or schedule a consultation with a qualified SEO consultant. Determine what issues can be fixed now, and come up with a plan and timeline to address coding and layout improvements, competitive positioning, and other on- and off-page ranking factors.

---

58  Neil Patel, How To Perform an SEO Audit – Free $5000 Template Included, http://www.quicksprout.com/2013/02/04/how-to-perform-a-seo-audit-free-5000-template-included/

During this process, a professional will analyze your website from many angles. Keyword opportunities will be discovered and analyzed, along with the state of your website's URL structure. The titles and subtitles on each page will be examined, as well as each page's meta-data.

Once this is done, your site's internal and external links will be analyzed, and your images will be checked for the optimization of *Alt tags*. An *alt tag* is HTML code that enables you to tell the search engines what words to associate with an image. Other relevant factors like duplicate site content, broken links, code quality, mobile-friendliness, and page load speed are all taken into account.

Finally, your SEO expert will look at your backlink profile for quality and risk potential, assess your authority and trust scores, and review your site's social media signals. [59] At the end of this process, a competitive backlink analysis should be conducted to see where your site stands in relation to the competition.

This may all sound like gibberish to you, but it's really just the tip of the iceberg. A full analysis of your website will reveal architectural, performance, and search engine issues that need to be resolved. Getting your sites' on-page SEO fundamentals in order can be a grind, but that upfront investment is crucial for long-term SEO performance.

## SEO-Friendly Code: Getting Under the Hood

It is important to build a website with SEO-friendly code in mind. Search engines are constantly crawling the web and interpreting page content. [60] What they see is not always what you see. There are many technical elements involved in SEO that contribute to your website's ranking success.

Your content must be indexable, and your website's link structures should be crawlable. Keywords are especially critical. You need to know

---

59 Steve Webb, How To Perform The World's Greatest SEO Audit, https://moz.com/blog/how-to-perform-the-worlds-greatest-seo-audit

60 Chapter Four, The Basics of Search Engine Friendly Design and Development, https://moz.com/beginners-guide-to-seo/basics-of-search-engine-friendly-design-and-development

which ones are most important and how to naturally weave them into your site and page content.

Technical SEO has evolved into its own genre of website coding. Unfortunately, some aspects of SEO will be out of reach for many entrepreneurs. Most businesses are going to need outside help to get a fully optimized website. While you might not know how to implement all of the recommended SEO coding tweaks for your site, we can still show what they are. Moz publishes the *Web Developer's SEO Cheat Sheet*,[61] which is a fantastic resource for SEO-friendly website development:

## https://moz.com/blog/seo-cheat-sheet

This cheat sheet is a notoriously useful tool for marketers and SEO experts alike. It clearly outlines what is important today and what has changed from previous versions.

On the first page of this guide, Moz outlines important HTML elements, HTTP status codes, canonicalization, and URL best practices. Page two is dedicated to Robot control syntax, important user agents, sitemap syntax, and pagination. Page three contains your social meta-data updates, *rich snippets*, and structured data inclusions. The final page outlines how you should target multiple languages and mobile web development. In 2015, the cheat sheet was updated with more than 100 changes. The user agent, social meta-data, and mobile web development sections were all updated with new information that designers and Internet marketers should know.

The largest change dealt with improving SEO with Structured Data and Schema markup.[62] This is a powerful form of SEO coding that is scarcely used, even by seasoned experts. Schema markup is part of your website code. It helps search engines return more informative results —

---

61  Cyrus Shepard, Announcing The Web Developer's SEO Cheat Sheet 3.0, https://moz.com/blog/seo-cheat-sheet

62  How TO Boost Your SEO By Using Schema Markup, https://blog.kissmetrics.com/get-started-using-schema/

and often extra information—for their users.

If you have ever seen *rich snippets* (and believe us, you have), you would have a better idea of how *structured data* and schema affect search results. A *rich snippet* is extra information you see in a search result, such as star ratings or event times. *Structured data* tells the search engine what your data means, not just what it says — therein lies the power. Adding the right schema markup to a web page defines the types of data elements on that page. The more a search engine understands about the context of your content, the more confidence it has to rank and display extra information about your website within its search results.

It also helps your search result stand out, improves your site's click-through-rate, and is likely to become a direct SEO ranking factor.[63]

For more information on structured data and schema, check out this blog post:

https://www.ducttapemarketing.com/blog/structured-data-schema/

## Optimizing a Web Page for SEO

Website layout is an important on-page ranking factor. As a website designer motivated to create SEO-friendly web designs, there are many things you can do to optimize the layout.

Search engines see web pages in a different way than visitors do, so you need to be sure to include all the right web page elements.

There are several on-page factors that should be considered for Google-friendly web design.[64] There are also specific areas for keyword placement that will enhance your ranking potential. Placing them

---

63  Barry Schwartz, Google May Add Structured Markup & Data To Ranking Algorithm. http://searchengineland.com/google-may-add-structured-markup-data-to-ranking-algorithm-230402

64  Cyrus, Shepard, More Than Keywords: 7 Concepts of Advanced On-Page SEO, https://moz.com/blog/7-advanced-seo-concepts?utm_content=buffer347a7&utm_medium=social&utm_source=linkedin.com&utm_campaign=buffer

appropriately in your titles, URLs, body text and alt tags is part of the process.

**Warning**: The next couple paragraphs are going to get a little more technical, but they will show you just how deep into the weeds Google will go to find and rank the best content.

*Keyword Density* refers to how many times a keyword is used in

 Synonyms play an important role in Googles searches. The search engine algorithm actively seeks out variants and synonyms to determine meaning and relevance on a page or set of pages. You can take advantage of this by using natural language variation in your content.

relation the rest of the text on the page, and it is important. If the keyword density is too low, your page may not carry enough weight to rank. If it's too high, your page will appear spammy and subject to an algorithmic penalty. Another measure is TF-IDF or *term frequency-inverse document frequency*. Google uses TF-IDF to measure how important a keyword is on your page, by comparing its frequency and usage on other pages.

*Page Segmentation* is about *where* on the page your keywords are placed. Placement is about selecting the right locations for keyword targets and it's just as important as your keyword choices themselves. Headers, footers, sidebars — these all have a distinct level of importance. Generally, the text, titles, and subtitles located in the main body of a page will have more weight than the rest of the page.

Google also uses *semantic distance* to determine the importance of your keyword choices. This is a fancy way of saying that Google looks at things like page formatting — such as a paragraph blocks or bullet lists — as a way to measure word relationships. Distance between words is measured to determine relational connection and relevance. *Semantic Distance* is yet another reason why you should consider using structured data and schema on your website. Schema markup enables you to tag page content in a way that provides semantic structure.

Other page layout elements beneficial for on-page SEO include:

- Social media links and share buttons
- Social media feeds
- A physical address located in the site footer
- An embedded Google Map
- Images, embedded videos, and podcasts

Keep in mind that Google penalizes sites that are top-heavy.[65] Put your best content above the fold, and resist the urge to use that space to bait and switch with ads or irrelevant content.

## SEO Keywords, Features, and Plugins

We have talked about the importance of keywords and how to locate and prioritize keywords for SEO. Now we need to discuss how to implement them on your website.

The first thing is your browser page title or title tag.[66] This is the most powerful tag on your website for establishing keyword relevance. These words often become the blue linked text in search results. It is also the best location to get a neat, concise description of the page content. Learning to use these appropriately will improve your SEO.

---

65  Barry Schwartz, Google Updates Its Page Layout Algorithm To Go After Sites "Top Heavy" With Ads, http://searchengineland.com/google-updates-page-layout-algorithm-go-sites-top-heavy-ads-183929

66  Rick DeJarnette, Nine Best Practices For Optimized &lt;title&gt; Tags, http://searchengineland.com/nine-best-practices-for-optimized-title-tags-111979

*Meta descriptions* are an indirect ranking factor but are still very important because they impact your *click-through rate* from the search results. Many SEO experts think that click-through rates are a heavily weighted ranking factor, while other studies have proven otherwise. In any case, your meta-descriptions need to be compelling. These are the gray and bold words in the search results.

You need to have a decent amount of web page copy, or Google will not see the page as valuable enough to rank. Typically, you need a minimum of 250 words on your home page, 350 words on your core service pages, 500 words on your blog posts, and a variety of in-depth posts of 1,000-2,500 words peppered throughout your website.

The purpose of *anchor links* is to link to relevant website content. Any external pages that you link to should be high quality, trustworthy, and relevant to your page content. You should also cross-link to other pages of your own website as appropriate.

In terms of images, Google cannot see your image content, but it can read your alt tags. You already know that an alt tag assigns a keyword to your image, but these should be relevant to the image, not just used to stuff another keyword on the page. All images should also have a title tag, which can be useful for your users as they hover through the site.

In *WordPress*, there are many core features and free plugins that will help you optimize the above elements for SEO. Yoast SEO, for example, is a plugin that can help you optimize page by page and site wide. In order for this plugin to be effective, you have to know your keywords. So once again, it all comes back to developing a highly targeted list of keywords.

An SEO plugin can help you set your browser names and descriptions, sync your keywords in the right places and give you real-time data on your keyword density. It will help you build a *search engine XML sitemap* — a code-level file that assists search engines in locating and tracking your pages and lets them know how often they should check your site for updates.

## Expert To Watch: *Joost de Valk*[67]

There are few people who have contributed as much to the field of website SEO as Joost de Valk. One of the first people to recognize that the average user could improve her SEO rapidly with only a few simple tweaks, Joost created the Yoast SEO plugin for WordPress to make SEO accessible to everyone

As a developer, online marketer, and SEO expert, Joost began his career working for several companies, ranging from enterprise hosting companies to online marketing agencies. He connected and worked with some of the largest businesses in the world when the SEO boom began.

In 2006, Joost founded CSS3.info, the largest CSS3 information resource on the Internet, which he sold in 2009. Back at it in 2010, he built Quix, a site that was featured in many prominent publications like *Mashable*, *ReadWriteWeb*, and *Lifehacker*.

Finally, in May 2010 Joost put all of his SEO knowledge to work and founded Yoast, a company that focuses on SEO consulting, WordPress optimization, and online marketing and content strategy. His many prestigious clients include eBay, Disney Interactive and the *Guardian*.

The Yoast SEO plugin, which boasts over ten-million users, was the most advanced plugin of its kind and catapulted Joost into the SEO hall of fame. Joost's team keeps it continually updated, so it is the best WordPress plugin of its kind.

A unique combination of developer, marketer, entrepreneur, and public speaker, Joost is passionate about SEO and using it to build stronger companies. Over the years, he has been invited to speak at many prominent events, including SES New York, SMX Munich, WordCamp Europe and many others. He speaks frankly about SEO, search engine marketing, and social media marketing.

---

67  About Joost de Valk, https://yoast.com/about-us/joost-de-valk/

Somehow, Joost still finds time to blog on his own web properties and on many prominent industry websites. We highly recommend that you take the time to subscribe to his free newsletter on Yoast.com and follow hime on Twitter @yoast.

# 09

# LINK BUILDING TODAY: THE DOS AND DON'TS

> *"There was a brief time in SEO history where you could build thousands of spam links and watch your site climb to the top of the first page. Those days are long gone. SEOs that do well today dedicate serious resources (time, money, and skilled labor) towards their link building campaigns."*
>
> Brian Dean, Backlinko

From the moment search engines rose to prominence, **backlinks** —links on third-party websites pointing back to your website — have played a major role in search engine rankings. Links include any clickable element on a third-party website that opens a page on your website when clicked.

There are many different types of backlinks and knowing what each does will serve you well. Here is a brief legend to help you understand some of them:

---

**BACKLINK LEGEND:**
- *Keyword anchor text:* "soft drink"
- *Generic anchor text:* "click here" or "read more"
- *Branded anchor text:* "Coca-Cola"
- *Raw URL text:* http://www.coca-cola.com
- **Linked images**

---

A healthy, natural backlink profile will typically contain a mix of all of the above backlink types.

Your *keyword anchor links* hold the most value because they are often directly tied to competitive search terms. These are a direct signals to Google, so they are very important. They also happen to be the most risky, as Google heavily scrutinizes *anchor links*, which can land you in a world of trouble if you have not closely followed the rules.

Until a few years ago link building was a volume game. Search engines counted each link as a vote, so the more votes you got, the better. As time went on, SEO service providers found creative methods of generating as many backlinks as possible for their client websites. If you had loads of links, it was easy to rank well. From then on, Google has been playing a cat-and-mouse game with the SEO industry. Google knew that these companies were exploiting algorithmic loopholes to benefit their customers and could not close these holes fast enough!

Eventually, these volume-based linking practices filtered into the Internet marketing mainstream. As recently as a few short years ago, it was quite common for Google to target large companies because of their extreme ranking manipulation techniques. JC Penny serves as a great example. [68]

The *New York Times* exposed JC Penny's link scheme, and Google

---

68  Vanessa Fox, New York Times Exposes JC Penny Link Scheme That Causes Plummeting Rankings in Google, http://searchengineland.com/new-york-times-exposes-j-c-penney-link-scheme-that-causes-plummeting-rankings-in-google-64529

responded harshly by announcing that JC Penny had violated webmaster guidelines and would be subject to a penalty. JC Penny's website promptly plummeted down in the search rankings.

The Penguin update, which we described earlier, was released shortly afterward. It was one of the hardest-hitting Google updates, targeting manipulative, unnatural backlinks. This was a punitive algorithm update that penalized companies using black hat SEO.

After the Penguin update, many Internet marketing companies had to reassess their strategies. Whereas they once hired offshore companies in places like India and Eastern Europe to outsource their SEO and web development, many of these agencies learned the hard way that this was not a sound strategy. Today, Internet marketing companies engage in much less offshore outsourcing, especially when it comes to SEO.

Backlinks are more important than ever, but now it is now less about quantity, more about quality and relevance.

In other words, the new golden rule of link building is: **A good backlink is one that you are proud of. You can justify why it is there based on the fact that it is was earned and not purchased.**

## The Ghosts of Backlinks Past

A large number of small business owners have seen their rankings tank over the last few years. This is because of the volume-quality change. Now, the vast majority of business owners who hired SEO consulting firms in the past feel like they've been burned.

SEO service providers have become the used car salesmen of the Internet. Thanks to obnoxious SEO firms that constantly misrepresent their services and still actively use black hat SEO techniques, most business owners ignore them altogether. No one wants to partner with a bad SEO company that will end up ruining his position on Google.

If you were one of the many business owners that used search engine optimization services in recent years, you are also probably feeling burned right now. This may be because you hired a cold-calling SEO company or one that sent you an unsolicited business email. Perhaps you hired an offshore link building service or even a domestic Internet marketing company. You may have even hired an SEO expert from a freelance website or from Craigslist.

If you purchased any type of link building or SEO package over the last few years, you may be one of the many disillusioned that lost money from shady or ineffective SEO services. It's even worse if you are realizing this for the first time right now. For a quick and easy way to check, go to Google Search Console.[69]

---

**QUICK TIP**

Navigate to Google Search Console (Previously Google Webmaster Tools):

**https://www.google.com/webmasters/**

If your site has already been added to Search Console, you can check the external links pointing to your website and even download the list. This is a free way to audit your backlink profile and use your common sense to judge the benefit or risk of each third-party link pointing to your site. Be sure you are sitting down, you may be in for a little surprise by the amount and quality of links pointing back to your site.

---

Inside your Search Console, you will see all of the backlinks to your website that Google is tracking and counting. Viewing this data for the first time can be an eye-opening experience for business owners who are not accustomed to seeing their website through Google's eyes. You may

---

69  Barry Schwartz, Google Webmaster Tools Rebrands To Google Search Console, http://searchengineland.com/google-webmaster-tools-rebrands-to-google-search-console-221282

not have been hit with a penalty yet, or you may be surprised to find a message from Google in your Search Console message center notifying you of a *manual penalty* or other SEO-related issue.

You could be a Penguin update away from losing all of your current rankings and online sales. That is why you need to rid yourself of any algorithmic time-bombs on your website. There are ways that you can tell Google not to count certain low-quality backlinks pointing to your website — you just need to find them first.

Search Console is a very important tool for SEO, and we will go into even more detail about it in Chapter 14. For now, we will discuss one important way of using Search Console to address risks and penalties related to backlinks.

This method of marking bad backlinks involves Google's own disavow tool.[70] Google allows you to mark the links that you do not want counted. Google does not want you to use the disavow tool until you have asked a website to remove the unwanted backlink. If the webmaster of the site does not agree, or does not respond, Google recommends using its disavow tool. This is an advanced SEO tactic and should not be used by a novice, as the

**WARNING**
Use at your own risk or, better yet, consult a professional.

tool can damage your website's search potential if used incorrectly.

First you will need to create your own audit spreadsheet of links. You can download these from Google Search Console. Since Google Search Console does not report new links immediately, you may want to consider generating more up-to-date link reports from premium SEO tools such as Majestic.com, Opensiteexplorer.org, or Ahrefs.com, which will show newly acquired backlinks. Compile all of the backlinks

---

70  Marie Haynes, Your Start-To-Finish Guide To Using Google's Disavow Tool, https://moz.com/blog/guide-to-googles-disavow-tool

you can find into a single spreadsheet.

The goal is to disavow all links from spammy domains. So your next step is to break down these URLs to their root or subdomain level. Do this by creating a second spreadsheet column and entering in the root domain for each link, for example:

1. Spammy link page: http://spamsite.com/spammy-page

2. Spammy root domain: spamsite.com

The next step is to audit your links. This is the part where you (or your SEO service provider) make the decision as to whether or not to disavow each link.

Once you have sorted out which links to disavow, you will disavow them by adding the term "domain" in front of each name:

**domain:spammysite.com**

With these disavow directives in place, you can save the document as a text file. You will need to provide Google with your disavow file by navigating to the Search Console disavow tool and selecting your site from the dropdown list.

Clicking on the "disavow links" button gives you the opportunity to upload your text file. A successful upload will result in a notification telling you exactly how many links you have disavowed from your website's backlink profile.

## Quality, Relevance, Trust, and Authority

Building high-quality backlinks is a big part of the game. Knowing how to find and secure these organic links can do amazing things for your rankings. There is too much risk and liability with link building shortcuts. It's just not worth it.

Recently, some SEO companies have been using *Private Blog Networks (PBNs)* to get more off-page SEO ranking points. These are large networks of standalone websites and blogs that look and act like real sites but are artificially created in large quantity to manipulate search engine rankings. Unscrupulous SEO companies charge clients for links to their web pages from these PBN sites, and while they have been effective, it is only at great risk. As you would expect, Google has responded with a heavy hand by targeting and de-indexing (i.e., blacklisting) or penalizing sites that use this form of link scheming. [71]

In terms of link building, SEO service providers now focus on four key factors — quality, relevance, trust, and authority. The SEO industry is finally taking Google's philosophy to heart. It's all about the user![72]

Before you start trying to earn quality links, look at your own website. Are you making an effort to create authoritative content? Your website needs to be organized efficiently, and it needs to provide useful information.[73]

You also need to promote your website content to get people to view and share it. Google will reward you if social sharing results in high quality, natural backlinks. The key to this process is writing useful content consistently and sharing it through a blog.

Experts are now saying that 90% of your efforts should be focused on great content and only 10% on link building.[74] Why? Because great content naturally attracts the best kinds of links.

If you proactively target a third-party website for a backlink opportunity, always assess the site's domain authority and relevance before taking any action. But the best method is still focusing on producing quality for your own website — your content will naturally attract the safest and most valuable kinds of links.

---

71  Barry Schwartz. Google Targets Sites Using Private Blog Networks With Manual Action Ranking Penalties. http://searchengineland.com/google-targets-sites-using-private-blog-networks-manual-action-ranking-penalties-204000

72  Google Company. Ten things we know to be true. https://www.google.com/about/company/philosophy/

73  Neil Patel, How To Build High Quality Backlinks In a Scalable Way, http://neilpatel.com/2014/12/30/how-to-build-high-quality-backlinks-in-a-scalable-way/

74  Neil Patel. How to Build High Quality Backlinks in a Scalable Way. http://neilpatel.com/2014/12/30/how-to-build-high-quality-backlinks-in-a-scalable-way/

## Methods of Power Link Building

Now that you know what kind of links to get and which ones to avoid, it's time to talk about where and how to get them.

 You and your SEO team should focus on employing modern power link building techniques that are in line with Google's overall mission and guidelines. Think of link building as networking, since it requires outreach and relationship building.

### #1: Major directory and review websites

Should you still place your website on major directories and review websites? Yes! Get your website listed with a full company profile on all major directory and review sites. BUT avoid spammy and low-quality directories at all costs.

### #2: Chambers of Commerce sites and business association sites

If your business is active in local chambers of commerce, or is a member of professional associations, you can take advantage of that connection online. These sites tend to have a lot of trust and credibility with Google, thus links from them are desirable.

### #3: Educational and government websites

If your company is associated with any educational institutions or government websites, you have a great opportunity to get a backlink from them. These sites have real domain authority and will help support your natural link building strategies.

### #4: Charity and non-profit websites

If your company supports, donates to, or volunteers with any charity or non-profits, add them to your link building profile. These organizations are often more than happy to add your link or logo to their site or to mention you in a blog or social media post. Often, all you have to do is ask.

## #5: Outbound guest blogging

Submit content on third-party websites that is high quality and relevant to your niche. If you can leverage their audience for traffic and sales, then you should be publishing semi-regular posts to establish links back to your website (often via an author attribution at the end of the post) and generate traffic. Guest blogging is still a great way to supplement link building when it is done selectively and strategically, but it is dangerous to rely on as your sole traffic- or backlink generating technique.

## #6: Inbound guest blogging

Invite people from other websites and publications to provide you with fresh, relevant content that is useful for your audience, and publish this content on your blog. Note: you want *exclusive* content, NOT permission to re-publish existing content. Variety will encourage traffic, and relevance will mean better quality backlinks for your website.

## #7: Social networks

Each of your social media profile pages has a link to your website. You can obtain high-value backlinks just by having an optimized presence on some key platforms.

## #8: Create infographics

Infographics are graphic pictorials that tell a story. They are an excellent way to include third-party sources in one piece of content, and they have a tendency to attract many links.

### #9: Broken link building

Search and find links on third-party sites that link to a page that no longer exists online. [75] Then create a post for that specific page — reach out to the site owner and replace the broken link with yours. You do them a service. You gain a valuable backlink. Boom. This is an advanced, but highly effective, link building technique.

### #10: Competitor analysis

Knowing what links your competitors have can make your campaigns better in more ways than one. In fact, this is so important, we dedicated the next section to it.

## Competitor Backlinks: The Analysis

A competitor analysis is an excellent way to capitalize on all of the hard work that your competition has put into achieving high rankings on Google. There are dozens of tools that can help you quickly and easily find and list your competitor's backlink profile, enabling you to copy the best parts of their footprint.

You can even find out whether or not certain backlinks have the potential to pass SEO ranking value or if they contain special code instructing Google not to count them for SEO. This is the difference between *"nofollow links"* and **standard links**. Here is a brief definition of each:

- *A standard link:* A link that passes SEO value — also referred to as **link juice** — from the sending page to the receiving page. As a result, these kinds of links from high- quality, relevant third-party websites can contribute to better search engine rankings.
- *A nofollow link:* A link that clicks to another web page, but has special code instructing search engines not to pass link juice (SEO value) from one page to another.

---

75 Anthony D Nelson, Broken Link Building Guide: From Noob To Novice, https://moz. com/blog/broken-link-building-guide-from-noob-to-novice

The nofollow attribute exists for a good reason. [76] It did a lot to ward off SEO spammers that were dumping URL nonsense onto the Internet, such as blog comment spam. Nofollows are used to deter spam in comments, forums, and other forms of user-generated content. Paid links are another great example. You can get links from high-authority sites by paying as an advertiser, such as a simple graphic ad on a third-party site that is linked back to your website. Since you paid for that link, and did not earn it by providing valued content, the publisher is supposed to nofollow the link back to your site so that you do not unfairly get SEO value through a link that you paid for.

On the front end, standard and nofollow links look no different to the user but they can appear very different to Google. Here is what the website code behind a clickable link for the word "Search for Growth" might look like.

---

**FOLLOW AND NOFOLLOW LINKS**

Here is a standard link that passes SEO juice:

`<a href="https://seoforgrowth.com">SEO For Growth</a>`

Here is a link with nofollow code that tells Google not to pass on any SEO value:

`<a rel="nofollow" href="https://seoforgrowth.com/">SEO For Growth</a>`

---

76  Megan Marrs, Follow Links Vs. No Follow Links: Should You Care?, http://www.wordstream.com/blog/ws/2013/07/24/follow-nofollow-links

You do want to have some nofollow links pointing to your website. Some SEO experts believe that they carry some direct SEO weight. Regardless, we believe that they carry a lot of indirect SEO value because of the targeted traffic and residual SEO signals that you get from nofollow links, particularly from high-authority, relevant websites.

Two of our favorite tools for competitor analysis are Ahrefs.com and SEMRush.com. Using these will enable you to step into the domain of your competitors so that you can access detailed profiles and data about their strategies. Then you can glean insight from them and use the information to strengthen your own content and backlinking strategies.

## How to Monitor Backlinks

If backlinks are so important to your rankings, how do you monitor them? As we explained earlier, Google Search Console has solved that problem for you. It is free to use and will provide you with all of the links that point to your website. Access to this information is incredibly valuable.

However, Google Search Console is not as fast at detecting new links as some other commercial tools. And the Search Console will not necessarily give you data or insight on other factors, like how many social signals were received from the page that hosts your backlink, if a backlink is standard or nofollow, or what the domain authority of the referring website might be.

In the post-Penguin era of SEO, it is important that all website owners keep regular watch on their backlink profile. [77] Links are important for gaining and maintaining search engine rankings, and they come loaded with penalty risk — far more than they ever have before. It may be worth your while to invest in a backlink monitoring service.

These services check for "barnacle links" that you acquire naturally

---

[77] Peter Van Der Graaf, Backlink Monitoring: Keeping Track of Your Existing Links, http://searchenginewatch.com/sew/how-to/2271355/backlink-monitoring-keeping-track-of-your-existing-links

and help you stay on the lookout for negative SEO links (malicious competitors trying to trigger a Penguin penalty on your site). With a sound content marketing plan in place, your site and blog posts will naturally attract links from quality sites via social sharing and reference links.

Additional business opportunities also become available to you when you monitor your links. You can see who has connected to your site, and this can open new doors and lead to real relationships.

## Expert to Watch: *Neil Patel*[78]

Neil Patel is one of the brightest lights in digital marketing. Known for his consistently incredible content and advice, as well as his skill with building and selling extraordinary analytics companies, Neil has been creating some of the best content in the industry for years.

In 2005, Neil was named one of the top influencers on the web by the *Wall Street Journal*. But perhaps his greatest accolade to date is being named a top 100 entrepreneur under the age of 30 by President Obama.

Neil has successfully built several multi-million dollar companies like Crazy Egg and Kissmetrics from scratch, all while running their influential blogs. He has won many awards for his blogging and has also been published in numerous online publications including *Inc.*, *Forbes*, *Entrepreneur*, *TechCrunch*, and *Fast Company*.

Through his companies and his blogging, Neil has developed deep knowledge of SEO, content marketing and conversion rate optimization.

With all of Neil's success in digital marketing, it doesn't make sense not to follow him. We strongly advise that you subscribe to the Kissmetrics, NeilPatel.com and QuickSprout blogs, and Neil will make sure that you always have the scoop on SEO and online marketing. Be sure to follow Neil on Twitter @neilpatel.

---

78  Neil Patel, http://www.quicksprout.com/about/

# MANAGING REPUTATION AND REVIEWS

*"Everybody with a website now is also a publisher. With Facebook and Twitter, brands have an opportunity to turn around customer experiences and make a bad situation into something much better. If you rock peoples' world, they will share that with people, and that enables your SEO."*

Dennis Goedegebuure, The Next Corner

What could be more important than your online reputation? With so many easy ways for customers to provide feedback on products and services, you cannot afford to ignore reputation management. A few thoughtless reviews can wreck your company.

Pound for pound, online reviews may be the most valuable of all SEO-ranking factors. We say this because the links and the actual text content of genuine reviews all contribute to SEO rankings. Not to mention, good reviews help you close more sales.

We guarantee that even if you shun every other piece of advice in this book, this tactic will still pay dividends. Committing to a professional, ongoing reputation-management strategy is imperative. If implemented correctly, you will eventually see a substantial increase in your web-based lead flow and sales.

**Here is a sample list of reviews sites to target for SMBs:**

**Critically Important**
- Google+
- Yelp

**Very Important**
- LinkedIn
- Facebook
- BBB
- Angie's List
- Thumbtack
- Yahoo Local
- Your Website

**Notable**
- CitySearch
- Judy's Book
- InsiderPages
- Manta
- Merchant Circle
- Local.com
- Kudzu

**NB Niche Review Sites:**
- Avvo — Lawyers
- TripAdvisor — Travel
- Healthgrades — Doctors
- Vitals — Doctors
- Houzz — building and remodeling contractors

When a consumer initiates an Internet search for a product or service, **he is already sold!** All he wants is a definitive reason to choose you over everyone else. He wants to see the "no-brainer" choice. Google Search gets you in front of your ideal customers during the purchase process. Online reviews and testimonials close the deal.

In 2014, Search Engine Land reported that 88% of consumers trust online reviews as much as they trust personal recommendations. [79] A mind-blowing 85% of consumers read up to ten online reviews before making a final decision to book an appointment or buy something.

Online reviews should be seen as the new referrals. Most of us will simply not make a purchase based on word-of-mouth referral alone. When a friend, neighbor, or business associate refers you to a service provider, the first thing that you do is follow up on that referral with a comprehensive Google search to validate those claims.

This "social proof" is a hot commodity online right now. Having dozens or hundreds of positive reviews is a superb way of entrenching yourself in the market. People trust regular people far more than they trust marketers or SEO experts. They would sooner hear from a random stranger about your company than they would from you.

## The Holy Grail of SEO

There is nothing better than being in the top Google spots for competitive search terms. Except perhaps being on top with dozens of more positive reviews than your next closest competitor. This closes the online sales loop. First they find you. Then they quickly recognize that you are better than everyone else. Then they buy from you.

There is no better local lead generator than a top organic ranking backed by a solid, authentic pool of positive online reviews with visible star ratings right on the search result page. It makes your competitors

---

79   Myles Anderson, 88% of Consumers Trust Online Reviews As much As Personal Recommendations, http://searchengineland.com/88-consumers-trust-online-reviews-much-personal-recommendations-195803

look foolish and bad at the Internet.

When people see that Google has crowned you with a top rank, and your clients have raved about your products and services again and again online, you become the logical choice. In fact, these signals are so persuasive that consumers become afraid to buy from anyone else. You become the safest. The best. The most recognized. And the only real choice.

This magic power enables you to quickly justify your pricing, while at the same time eliminating the risk of attracting low ballers and cheapskates.

The holy grail of local SEO is your ability to unite the forces of ranking well with the equally powerful force of consumer review data.[80] It is like saying, "I am the best," without ever having to say a word. The high rank and consumer sentiment says it for you in a well-orchestrated, seamless marketing technique straight from the search engine results pages (SERPS).

As explained earlier, Google's Pigeon update merged map results with traditional ranking factors. This means you can now affect your Google local search engine rankings and online reputation management more than ever before.

Online reviews improve conversion rates. Highly rated companies tend to get the most business. For a small business or a startup that desperately needs credibility, what could be better? Individually, SEO rankings and online reviews are very powerful, but when you combine the two with an effective website, you create a *lead generation* machine like no other. The control lies in your own hands. All you have to do is take advantage of this opportunity Google has given you.

---

80  George Aspland, Local Businesses: How To Get Good Online Reviews That Build Business, http://searchengineland.com/local-businesses-get-good-online-reviews-build-business-214939

## Your Online Review Strategy

Online reviews, and the systems that drive them, are rigged against your business. Without an online review strategy, you cannot encourage positive reviews or counter negative ones.[81] An unmonitored stream of online reviews could be costing you a fortune right now, and you would never even know it.

Consumers expect to get great products and services at a fair price. But this does not necessarily mean that they will take extra time out of their busy days to find your *online review profile* and gush about how great you are. If everyone reviewed all the products and services they used on a daily basis, there would not be time to eat, sleep, or take a shower.

On the other hand, if you screw up and give your customer a bad experience, prepare for the wrath of the Olympians! He would be glad to spend all sorts of extra time making sure that you get a bad review, not just on one site, but on several. Just in case.

Review sites have always been rigged to collect negative reviews. Why? Because they are more entertaining on almost every level — to read, to write, and to share. Good news is boring, but bad news is real news to the Internet. It is the same reason why mainstream news stories on television are often negative. This is the Internet's version of gawking and rubbernecking.

This means that if you do not take the necessary steps to protect and manage your online reputation, it will manage you. To thrive in the online space, in this dynamic search engine economy, you need to work reputation management into your daily routine.

---

81 Caroline Skipsey, Marketing: What's Your Strategy For Dealing With Online Reviews?, https://www.brandwatch.com/2015/05/the-power-of-online-reviews-whats-your-brand-strategy/

**QUICK TIP** An online review strategy can be part of your brand management plan or process. The ability to listen to what is being said about you online gives you the opportunity to respond appropriately. A resolved negative comment is far less potent than one that goes unanswered. Companies like yours need to be present to deal with the repercussion of online reviews.

## Managing Your Online Reputation

There are a lot of bad practices in the industry where online reputation is concerned. Without a strong online reputation, your business will lose a lot of opportunity online. You need a strong offense and defense to succeed in this corner of the Internet.

Here are eight tips and tactics for an effective online reputation management strategy. To avoid any holes in your lead generation system, make sure that these are part of your plan.

1. Never, ever write, buy, or encourage fake reviews. [82] They just aren't worth it. They look fake, they sound fake, and your review account is worth too much to risk being shut down because of underhanded practices. Plus, you never know about Google in the future. They could develop a way to tell the difference, and then where would you be?

2. Be smart about asking your customers for appropriate feedback. Do NOT ask all of them for feedback at the same time or you

---

82  Shawn Hessinger, Managing Your Online Reviews Ain't Easy – But We Can Change That, http://smallbiztrends.com/2014/09/managing-your-online-reviews.html

may attract more negative backlash than you planned for. And many sites will flag you for soliciting reviews. Yelp is notorious for this.

3. Develop a routine with simple instructions. Print out a basic feedback form on a business card, for example. This will help you collect feedback for your website.

4. When asking for feedback, make sure to ask your client to mention the product or service they used. Detailed reviews containing keywords are far more valuable than generic ones. They read well and give you additional ranking credit for the content of the review.

Example:

"*They did a great job!*"

is not as valuable as:

"*This web development agency did a great job on our web design project. They are masters at search engine optimization and WordPress website development.*"

5. Collect reviews on your website first. This is a great way to intercept negative sentiment before it goes live to the world. It gives you time to address the problem and convert a negative experience into a positive one. There are many excellent WordPress review plugins that make collecting and moderating reviews directly on your website a simple process.

6. Create a custom online review funnel. This is similar to the online review plugin mentioned above, but a review funnel has its own URL and is super easy to use. What does a custom online review funnel look like? Check this one out:

### http://seoforgrowth.reviews

7. Always engage with your reviewers. Review response is underrated, yet it has been proven to help convert negative

reviews into positive ones for your company.

8. Do not panic about negative reviews. ALWAYS take the high road and respond professionally. Never engage in a full-on battle with a customer online. You will come off looking like the villain and will only make things worse.

## Becoming a Brand Publisher

Thanks to the world of online customer reviews, you need to become a brand publisher. Building your brand online and building your online reputation are really the same thing. You, and everyone in your company, are responsible for reputation management.

This is because your company is your brand, and your brand is your online reputation. Your brand, in fact, is the sum total of all of your marketing efforts. From your website to blogs and social media, and yes, to online reviews.

A competent brand publisher understands that there is a great need to monitor and manage consumer sentiment. Your brand needs to be uniform inside and out.

Not all complaints will be solvable, but if you try hard enough, you can turn many of those lemons into lemonade. Wherever you can, invite further discussion with your customer on a private platform, like email. Be creative about solving her problems and as helpful as you can be. Most people just want to know that you did your best.

Don't let your consumers catch you using bad SEO practices.

This will cause a misalignment, and you will be attacked. You cannot control what people say about your brand, but you can plan for the inevitable. [83] As a general rule, everyone in your company needs to behave like a publisher. What they do impacts your bottom line.

You cannot, for example, have an employee that says horrible things about your clients on their social media pages. Especially when you frame yourself as a friendly, reliable company. Keep things consistent. Set goals and policies, and do not deviate from your brand ideology.

It is also important to be active and honest as a brand publisher. Being honest means inviting transparency into your company and never being afraid to apologize if something goes wrong.

Brand publishers must also realize that vigilance is key when public sentiment is involved. If you are paying attention, you can prevent or remedy most negative content on the Internet about you. This will go a long way toward ensuring that your brand continues to grow and thrive online.

## Content to Credibility to Conversion

The online review arena is easy to understand for brand publishers like you. All credible review content results in a conversion or the opposite of a conversion — a missed sale. That is why it is your job to make sure that the content published about your company is positive.

You can ensure this by stimulating your own content marketing machine so that your brand publishes positive content about your products and services. This content may not be as potent as third-party reviews, but it can still persuade a customer into thinking that a handful of negative reviews were the exceptions, not the rule.

You can begin your online review strategy by reaching out. Ever heard the saying, "You have to write reviews to get reviews?" Your company can build your brand online by giving reviews to companies

---

83  Gini Dietrich, Seven Tips To Building Your Brand's Reputation Online, http://www.inc.com/theupsstore/seven-tips-to-building-your-brands-reputation-online.html

in your existing partner and referral network.[84] These relationships are important, and what helps them, will help you.

Then you can build an initial book of reviews for yourself. Sometimes giving a review first is all it takes. Social networking sites like LinkedIn are amazing at generating reciprocal reviews for your company. Focus your efforts on Google and LinkedIn first, then expand to other platforms.

---

**Navigate to:**

**https://www.google.com/business/**

QUICK TIP   Google My Business places your business information on search, maps, and Google+ so that customers can find you no matter what device they happen to be using.

---

Many review websites will demand more time and effort than LinkedIn, but the point is to focus on the acquisition of positive content. Good reviews are a credibility goldmine and they will contribute to sales growth over time.

## Leveraging Google+ and Google My Business

Of all the social networks online, Google+ is the most underrated, underutilized, and misunderstood. It is an extremely powerful social platform and the single most important network for search engine optimization. Just using Google My Business boosts the local SEO potential for your business. You need to leverage Google+ and Google My Business right now.

---

84   Brenda Bernstein, How To Maximize Your LinkedIn Endorsements, http://www.socialmediaexaminer.com/manage-linkedin-endorsements/

Your Google My Business page needs to be augmented with the best SEO practices. [85] Here are some important tips. Fill out as much of the profile info as possible:

- ✓ Enter your correct business location so that it is marked on the map.
- ✓ Add your opening and closing times and your payment options.
- ✓ List your business website.
- ✓ In the Story section, add a Tagline and a 200-300+ word Introduction about your company. Include 2-3 anchor links back to your website, including an inner page or a blog post.
- ✓ In the Links section, add your website, YouTube Channel and links to all of your social media pages.
- ✓ Select the business categories that are most appropriate.
- ✓ Add your logo and a custom background image.
- ✓ Choose specific categories over broad ones to help Google.
- ✓ Encourage customers to review your company from your Google Maps listing page.
- ✓ Add unique text posts to your Google+ Posts section.
- ✓ Add image and videos.
- ✓ Follow other Google+ users and Google+ company pages.
- ✓ Follow some relevant Google+ communities and consider creating your own community.
- ✓ Add the Google+ badge to your website (**https://developers. google.com/+/web/badge/**).
- ✓ Make sure you complete the verification process. On initial setup, this involves a PIN code that Google physically mails to your business address.
- ✓ Make posting to your Google My Business page part of your social media regimen.

---

85  Optimize Your Business Information, https://support.google.com/business/answer/4454429?hl=en

✓ Invest in a Google Street View virtual tour (**https://www.google.com/maps/streetview/trusted/**).

Customers will be able to review your company on your Google My Business maps listing by clicking on the "write a review" button. Don't forget to encourage your customers to provide some details as to the product purchased or service performed to increase the chance that keywords are naturally included in their review copy.

## Expert to Watch: *Mark Traphagen*[86]

Like many SEO experts today, Mark Traphagen started out quite accidentally, after he was assigned to figure out how to create online success for his employer. Despite his lack of experience, he created a profitable online store that was competitive against one of the biggest sites in the world. Today, he is the Senior Director of Marketing for Stone Temple Consulting, one of the most respected SEO companies in the world.

Mark has a very strong personal brand, 140,000 social media followers, and he is an in-demand public speaker on the SEO circuit.

He has spoken at industry conferences like SMX, PubCon and MozCon. A regular featured writer for major online publications, Mark's work can be found on Search Engine Land, Moz Blog, and on Marketing Land, where he writes a monthly column on social media.

We highly recommend joining Google+ and then following Mark. He has built an amazing identity on Google+ and knows how to leverage that platform for SEO better than anyone else right now. His Google+ page has been visited more than 48 million times and contains great information that will help you bridge the divide between social and SEO knowledge. If you speak to him directly on Google+, he almost always answers.

---

86  About Mark Traphagen, https://www.stonetemple.com/about-mark-traphagen/

Along with Eric Enge, Mark is one of the most progressive SEO experts in the field. Bookmark any articles of his that you come across. You will find yourself returning to them again and again. For more on Mark check out his well-maintained Twitter feed at @marktraphagen.

# 11

# SOCIAL MEDIA SEO INTEGRATION

*"When I hear people debate the ROI of social media? It makes me remember why so many businesses fail. Most businesses are not playing the marathon. They're playing the sprint. They're not worried about lifetime value and retention. They're worried about short-term goals."*

Gary Vaynerchuk, Vayner Media

Social media was not taken seriously for many years, and it was dubbed "a passing fad." Today we know that the opposite is true. Many celebrities and businesses have created digital empires using social media.

The relationship between social media and SEO is complicated. Search engine companies dispute that social media has any influence on SEO, but this runs contrary to SEO service providers' experiences in the field. This chapter reveals the true relationship between the social media and SEO and explains how they impact your brand's rankings.

## The SEO-Social Media Connection

Many in the industry claim that highly engaged content has much greater SEO value than content that is never clicked, shared, commented on, liked, or tweeted. But when directly asked, Google has flip-flopped in its response to this assertion. At one point it confirmed that social media was a ranking factor, but has denied it since.

On one hand, it wouldn't make much sense for Google to completely ignore social signals, because this is how users are starting to independently assess the value and quality of online content. On the other hand, Google cannot place too much dependence on social signals because they are in control of third party websites.

No one really knows how Google uses social signals to determine organic rankings. Although one recent study shows no correlation specifically between social sharing and content that receives backlinks, only one thing has been confirmed for certain — social signals are becoming more important with time. [87]

That's why we believe that social signals are super important for your website and for your business. Even if they do not have a direct impact on SEO, they certainly have an enormous indirect impact on your website's visibility.

These social signals can include the size of your communities on Google+, Facebook, Twitter, LinkedIn, Instagram, and other platforms. They can also include share and like ratios, and how many genuine fans and followers you have.

There are a myriad of indirect benefits from building your social media for SEO purposes. These include all of the inbound links, referral visits, and conversions that come directly from your social media posts. Viewers on your social platforms can click directly on to your website where the magic can happen. As a constant source of community traffic, social media is priceless.

---

87 Steve Rayson, Content, Shares, and Links: Insights from Analyzing 1 Million Articles, https://moz.com/blog/content-shares-and-links-insights-from-analyzing-1-million-articles

## Building Your Brand Community

Understanding how social signals impact your website SEO is important, even if they only indirectly affect your rankings. One of the main factors involved with this indirect impact concerns your brand community. Search engines like Google and Bing are taking community size into account as a method of measuring content value. This makes sense because it takes a lot of great content to build a large, authentic community of engaged people.

Let's address the obvious question on your mind. What about fake fans? Do they count? No they don't, because fake followers do not engage. It is not simply the size of the community that counts, but how active this community is on your pages. An authentic Facebook community of 8,000 people, for example, could result in hundreds of views and actions on your social posts each day, not to mention extending your reach through paid boosts.

When viewers finally reach your website, they may choose to engage with you on your blog, share your content, or sign up for a trial. Whatever they do, your website stats will improve, as will your engagement signals. Anything shared from your website is another opportunity to hook a new follower.

A large community with high-level engagement tells the world that you are a transparent brand willing to reach out to customers. It says a lot about your commitment to delivering great customer service and the best possible experience for your customers

Online brand-building techniques should be a major part of your overall SEO strategy.[88] Although we can't predict the future relationship between social signals and SEO, we know they are growing in importance as Google tries to determine authenticity and content value. And for that reason, they are an integral component of a holistic inbound marketing strategy.

---

88  Eric Enge, Do Social Signals Drive SEO?, 89Do Social Signals Drive SEO, http://www.convinceandconvert.com/digital-marketing/do-social-signals-drive-seo/

## Adding Keywords to Your Social Content

What about the social content itself? Don't social posts on Facebook and Twitter have some value as backlinks? Many marketers believe this to be true, despite Google's arguments to the contrary. There is a theory that search engines see web pages shared on social media sites as more valuable than those that are not shared.

In terms of link building, this would be true except for the fact that all social media posts contain nofollow links. Remember that extra code you can add to a link to tell Google not to use it in its ranking process? All social media sites use the nofollow tag as a matter of policy. This renders social media links less useful as a link-building technique. But, as you know by now, SEO is so much more than backlinks.

QUICK TIP

Community building may only be an indirect ranking factor, but it creates a cascade of win-wins and is right in line with Google's user-centric philosophy. Nurturing your social media channel is an excellent way to generate social signals and gain trust.

Social posts containing the right keywords get more visibility in that social network. [89] This means that you should treat social media networks as search engines. With the right keywords in your headings, posts, and hashtags, your social posts can rank for social media searches just like web pages do in Google searches.

---

89   Help Customers Find You: How To Use Keywords On Your Social Networks, https://blog.kissmetrics.com/help-customers-find-you/

**QUICK TIP** Use social SEO for the same reason you use traditional website SEO — to help people search for and discover your content. Today's SEO is about optimizing all of your digital content, not just your website content.

Keywords and hashtags on sites like Twitter, Facebook, and Instagram lead people to your content. This has enormous indirect SEO value. If a new fan on your Twitter page catches sight of a hashtag keyword that interests them, he can get pulled into the current of your inbound marketing. That single fan might, for example, click the hashtag and find other posts. He may share these posts. He could arrive at your blog and leave a comment there. He may even become a fan of yours on Facebook, which means he'll see the next thing you post as well. All of this engagement has him getting to know you a little better, which can spark the trust that leads to a sale.

Keywords are navigational tools. They should be used for on-site SEO on all of your social media pages. People using Facebook or another social media account might happen across your company because of the foundation-level keywords you built into your page. When it comes to search, keywords are the stepping stones that guide people to your content.

You should optimize your social media pages the same way that you optimize your website and Google My Business page. Place SEO keywords in headlines, summaries, links, biographies, and captions, as well as in the text itself. Getting ahead in SEO is as much about predicting trends as running with them. If you are a web designer or marketer, make sure that your client's SEO strategy includes social SEO.

## Creating a Network of Sharing

The good news is that content from social networks often appears in Google Search results.[90] The larger your community size and the more it shares your content, the more opportunity you have for additional search engine visibility. Your Facebook page and Twitter page can rank on Google.

The entire purpose or goal of a social network is sharing. Beyond likes and comments, sharing is easily the most significant action for SEO. This is because sharing functions on multiple levels for your company. It acts as a vote of confidence from your follower. It acts as a promotional tool for your company. And it helps to extend the reach of your network.

Within your social network, sharing becomes a commodity. For every piece of useful content that you post, some of your community members will choose to share it as well. As they do, people outside of your network — in your fans' networks — will see your posts and other content. This will attract more people to your brand and, eventually, bring them into your sales cycle.

Social media posts can end up in all sorts of places beyond social networks. They are being used in blog posts and articles, in eBooks and slideshow presentations. If you create content that other people want to reference, you can attract fans, backlinks, and traffic via these posts, as people link to your website.

This is in line with what Google wants for your brand. Google wants you to build a loyal following around great content. Technical website SEO is a big part of achieving that, but you can't get there without social media.

Traditional search engines are important, but so are social search engines, and they are where your repeat customers hang out. Google attracts people who are looking for a product or service *right now*. Social

---

90  Angie Pascale, 7 Legitimate Ways That Social Media Impacts SEO, http://www.clickz. com/clickz/column/2342211/7-legitimate-ways-that-social-media-impacts-seo

media enables you to stay in front of them until they decide to buy.

You already have a ton of fans out there, and they are already sharing. All you need to do is connect with them and maintain an SEO mindset when participating in social media. This is how you create and nurture a network of sharing that will boost your overall SEO visibility.

## Brand Awareness and Influence

Your social content machine is an SEO linchpin that will stimulate brand awareness and grow your community exponentially. Every genuine social community member has value. Social media does more to influence your buyers than just about anything else.

In order to strengthen your social SEO rankings, you will need to build brand awareness and influence. This is done by publishing optimized content on your social media pages in a strategic manner according to a calendar or campaign. [91] The content flow should be ongoing and it should be consistently measured, analyzed, and tweaked according to your findings.

**QUICK TIP** Consider the rules of SEO when crafting your social content. If your primary goal is to help find your business, you should be creating messages that make you stand out from the crowd. Keep your content smart, brief, and easy to enjoy at a glance. Most of all, make it irresistible!

---

91 Top-of-Funnel Marketing Tools: Content For Brand Awareness & SEO, http://www. brafton.com/blog/content-marketing/top-of-funnel-marketing-tools-content-brand-awareness-seo

You will need a social platform design that is in line with your brand identity. Your fans should be able to instantly recognize you as the author of a piece of content thanks to your creative design, ethos, and tone. You should always weave a strong, on-brand message into all your content so that it stands out from the crowd.

Think of a Facebook newsfeed. Does your post stick out from among the surrounding posts? Does it inspire awareness of your brand with just a glance? How does it influence your fans? It's great to have some fun, but time is money. Every piece of social content should align with your overall SEO strategy and marketing goals.

Creating engagement within a niche community is powerful. This is the true meaning of influence. By seeking out constant alignment with your followers, they will grow to know and trust your company as leading experts in the field. They will begin to look out for your content and will share it. Once you start building influencer status, even if it's within a smaller group, your content becomes inherently more valuable because it has your name is on it. Influence snowballs with each new high-quality piece of content you publish.

Focus your effort on your headlines, keywords, and calls to action. Engagement starts on social media, but, ideally, you want to attract your fans back to your website, which has been specially engineered to convert.

Your social media networks are critical for building your brand awareness and for exerting influence online. We predict that, in the next few years, social signals will become an official SEO ranking factor. For now, we see social media as an extension of SEO — an inbound marketing tactic that directly impacts your reach, popularity, brand identity, and influence online.

## Expert to Watch: *Chris Brogan*[92]

Chris Brogan is the CEO of Owner Media Group Inc., which provides

---

92  Chris Brogan, https://en.wikipedia.org/wiki/Chris_Brogan

people and corporations with business development and digital marketing advice. His clients include brands like Disney, Coke, Google, Microsoft, and Cisco. When he's not advising, Chris's company sells webinars, courses, books, and speeches on topics that improve business practices and personal leadership.

Chris is one of the most inspiring thought leaders in the digital marketing field today. He is a *New York Times* bestselling author, having already published eight books on modern Internet marketing, SEO, and social media, and a highly sought-after professional speaker on the marketing circuit who has delivered more than 1,000 speeches to brands all over the world. He has also appeared on the Dr. Phil show and has interviewed a number of affluent business people such as Richard Branson and Paulo Coelho. *Forbes* named Chris one of the Must Follow Marketing Minds of 2014, he was listed by Statsocial as a #3 power influencer online, and his website ranks among the 100 best websites for entrepreneurs.

Needless to say, Chris knows his stuff when it comes to content marketing and SEO. He has years of experience working with companies of all shapes and sizes, and has seen firsthand how the lines between SEO and social media have blurred. Chris's mission is to help people see and understand all that is now possible with online marketing in the social media age. He emphasizes the human connection in social media selling, which is a critical ingredient in your ability to understand how SEO and social work together online.

You should sign up for Chris's newsletter at ChrisBrogan.com and make sure that you visit his blog regularly for his fascinating insights into the industry. Chris has a way of humanizing his content, so it is easy to read and entertaining to follow. He is one of the most honest voices online right now, and he runs all of his own social media accounts! We also strongly suggest reading *Trust Agents* and *The Freaks Shall Inherit the Earth*. There is a lot of great information in those books about online entrepreneurship, selling, and how social communities work online today. Be sure to follow Chris on Twitter @chrisbrogan.

# SEO AWARENESS AND UPDATING

*"The best place to hide a dead body is on the second page of Google."*

Unknown

In the realm of search engine optimization, two more factors become critical to your ongoing success — awareness and updating. You need to stay on the Google treadmill and adjust your SEO tactics to keep rolling with their punches.

There is no end to search engine optimization. Thanks to the constant changes in this niche, there are always more tweaks and actions that you need to take to achieve and maintain organic rankings.

## The Importance of Current SEO Knowledge

In the legendary 1999 movie, *The Matrix*, Neo was asked whether he wanted to take the red pill or the blue pill. Each would irrevocably change his future. By reading this book, you have already taken the red pill! You know the truth about your website rankings and what really powers them online.

If you are new to SEO, you will never look at another website the same way again. In the meantime, the blue-pill website designers and business owners will continue to hobble along, ignoring modern SEO, and hoping for the best. In this new era of SEO, knowing the truth about the search engine economy is not enough.

Google will continue the two-ringed battle of improving the quality of its search engine results, while aggressively fighting web spammers. Trying to find and exploit the algorithmic loopholes is no longer viable for SEO.

As business owners that want to grow and as website designers that want to build effective, revenue-generating websites for clients, you must continue your SEO education and follow the blogs and industry websites that will provide you with the best insight and information on the industry.

A designer or business owner that does not understand "how the deck is stacked" cannot possibly hope to compete in a growing arena of best practices. Google wants businesses to optimize their websites fairly so that search engine users will be able to find the best possible content.

Take the time to read industry studies[93] and the best blogs written by key industry experts, and subscribe to the leading SEO media sites — this is how you can say ahead of the algorithmic curve. When it comes to SEO, the more in tune you are with the industry, the better you'll be at anticipating Google's next move.

## Who has the Best SEO Information?

In many ways this question is a difficult one to answer. Since SEO is now a content-driven pursuit, more industry folks have been pumping

---

93  The Ace Up Your SEO Sleeve, http://www.searchmetrics.com/knowledge-base/ranking-factors/

out content. Thus, there is too much content and too many sources to choose from.

Some people have large audiences and are perceived as experts, simply because they have managed to accumulate these audience numbers. Just because an individual is a great SEO journalist, does not mean that he can roll up his sleeves and create a solid SEO program that produces results. The person that wrote an insightful SEO blog post might not be able to rank themselves out of a wet paper bag. A real-world example might be Bob Costas, the sports commentator. He may be an amazing announcer, but he cannot play ball.

There are a lot of Kim Kardashian types in the SEO niche; they are "famous for being famous," but they are only rehashing the thought-leading content that the true industry influencers are producing from scratch.

 **QUICK TIP** A bustling blog about SEO is no indicator that the company in question is genuinely good at what it does. You should never neglect due diligence because of the content volume and community size that a company has managed to build over time. Results are results and blog posts are blog posts. Speaking about techniques is very different than employing them.

It is troubling that these great writers are also perceived as talented SEO experts, though there is no evidence to support that title. Then you have the reverse of this situation — the truly exceptional SEO minds who are too busy producing some of the most inventive and effective SEO strategies on the planet to blog about it.

These individuals are out on the front lines, working in boutique agencies or as independent consultants, and there is a good chance that you have never heard of them or read a single blog post they've written. [94] They don't have an audience, but they fight the good fight each day by doing SEO the right way and getting their clients websites to crush their competitors all year round.

We have been earning a living from Internet marketing and SEO-friendly web design for over a decade. We know who can play ball and who only thinks that they can. Often you will find that the best sites online are owned by SEO companies or experts who actively work in the field of SEO and publish their findings for their community to see.

If you come across a blog that belongs to a random person and there doesn't seem to be any evidence that he has worked in the field of SEO — caveat emptor, buyer beware! A lot of people take on work claiming to know what they are doing because they understand the theory. But there is a vast chasm of difference between a theory and a practice, with many lessons in between. In other words, just because you read it on the Internet, doesn't mean it's true.

## Which Blogs and Websites to Follow Today

In addition to experts we've been recommending at the end of each chapter, there are a number of excellent websites and blogs that you should start to follow to keep your SEO edge. Here is our personal list of the best places online to source SEO information that is reliable and progressive.

### For Up To the Minute News:
*Search Engine Roundtable*
https://www.seroundtable.com

---

94  James A Martin, Top 10 Things To Look For In an SEO Expert, http://www.cio.com/article/2400260/careers-staffing/top-10-things-to-look-for-in-an-seo-expert.html

Barry Schwartz does an excellent job at *Search Engine Roundtable* (SER). There, he reports on what Internet marketers like us are discussing right now. Google's algorithm is top secret, and the company guards information when new updates are made. SEO consultants that handle and monitor large books of clients can often sense when Google is testing or has released a new update — well before anyone has written a blog post or follow-up story on the news. Search Engine Roundtable monitors and posts the SEO chatter from around the web. SER blog posts tend to generate a lot of discussion and debate from the SEO community.

Even setting up notifications from three or so of these sources can keep you informed enough to stay ahead of any new Google releases. This will give you time to anticipate, or react to, updates as quickly as possible.

While there can be some trolling, great insight and comments from the community make this a site worth tracking. These are people on the frontline, executing SEO strategies and tactics, not just writing about them. This is the best site around for real-time SEO information.

### For Weekly Industry News:

*Search Engine Land*

http://searchengineland.com

Danny Sullivan co-founded Search Engine Land (SEL), which has become the best place to source weekly round-up news, providing true value amidst all the clutter. From a mainstream marketing perspective, SEL does tend to break a lot of SEO stories, thanks to its website's popularity and long history of covering industry news.

SEL also publishes exclusive contributor content from some of the top SEO minds in the niche, including Eric Enge, Mark Traphagen, Glenn Gabe, Larry Kim, and dozens of others. Besides being the leading online SEO magazine for professionals, SEL provides some choice educational resources: webinars, guides, and conferences.

This is one of the best industry sites to follow because it presents the SEO industry in a way that relates to non-SEO business users as well as SEO pros. With the diverse range of content, you are sure to find information here that will benefit you.

## SEO News, Technical SEO, and In-Depth Articles

As you follow these industry sites, you will find that there is a lot of overlap in content coverage, with many other sites mimicking this content. The best content on these sites comes from contributors and staff writers who create in-depth articles on a particular aspect of search engine marketing and SEO.

### Search Engine Journal
**http://www.searchenginejournal.com**

Search Engine Journal (SEJ) has always been a great resource. Recently the website seems to have new life and energy, perhaps thanks to Executive Editor Kelsey Jones, founder Loren Baker, CEO Jenise Henrikson, Chief Social Media Strategist, Brent Csutoras, and the team they lead.

The thing we love most about SEJ is that most of the content comes from people in the industry who make their living from SEO consulting, rather than SEO journalism.

The website is a solid mix of top-name SEO contributors like Roger Montti, Larry Kim and Danny Goodwin, and you get really great posts from mainstream SEO consultants as well. There are also good guides, events, and podcasts — we love the *Marketing Nerds* podcast!

### Search Engine Watch
http://searchenginewatch.com

Search Engine Watch (SEW) provides tips and information about searching the web, analysis of the search engine industry, and help for site owners trying to improve their ability to be found on the search engines. That is their mission statement. SEW has been an industry fixture for years and is another great SEO resource.

### The SEM Post
http://www.thesempost.com

The SEM Post is another one of our favorite resources. Jennifer Slegg, a well-known and long-time industry expert, is the founder of The SEM Post. She was previously with Search Engine Watch and ClickZ and has been writing about the industry for over fifteen years. The SEM Post has an amazing group of contributors including Ann Smarty, Greg Jarboe, and Stoney deGeyter.

### MOZ Publications
http://moz.com

Moz is perhaps the most well-known of all the SEO websites. There are a wide range of resources that can be used on this site, including SEO tools, vibrant in-house community engagement, a very educational blog, and a constant stream of fresh content.

This is one of the top resources for business owners, SEO beginners, and intermediate SEO consultants looking to round off their SEO knowledge.

Moz also runs **http://mozcast.com**, which is a weather report showing recent ranking turbulence in the Google algorithm. The hotter and stormier the weather, the more Google's rankings have changed.

## Keeping Up With Official Policies

There are few places where you are going to get the kind of accurate information that can be found on the *Google Webmaster Central Blog*. This is where Google makes all of its special announcements about changes to Google Search.

There are, in fact, two Google blogs that you should follow which will help you stay up to date on official Google documentation and algorithm changes. These are:

### Google Webmaster Central Blog
### http://googlewebmastercentral.blogspot.com/

Here you will find Google's *SEO Starter Guide*, which all new SEO service providers, web designers, and business owners should read. This is the official document in which Google outlines exactly what you can do in order to make your website better for SEO. It is definitely worth a read.

You can find it here:

### http://static.googleusercontent.com/media/www.google. com/en//webmasters/docs/search-engine-optimization-starter-guide.pdf

By following these official sources of information, you will always have a benchmark by which to gauge third-party information. This is important as third-party news and blog sites may contain more opinion than fact.

## Expert to Watch: *Rand Fishkin*[95]

Rand Fishkin is one of the most creative players in the SEO field today. After founding Moz as a "software as a service" company, Rand took the title Wizard of Moz. Moz sells inbound marketing and marketing analytics software subscriptions and has become one of the largest communities of digital marketers and SEO experts online.

Rand started in the world of SEO while he was still in college and SEO forums were the go-to content sources online. Since then, Rand

---

95   Rand Fishkin, https://moz.com/about/team/randfish

has attracted over a million subscribers, has spoken at nearly all of the major global SEO conferences, and has been invited to speak at Google, Facebook and Microsoft, among many other wildly influential companies.

Rand has also had great success co-authoring a pair of books on SEO. *The Art of SEO* (first and second editions) and *Inbound Marketing and SEO* have both been huge industry successes in their own right. He also wrote *The Beginners Guide to Search Engine Optimization*, which is among the most read pages on SEO today. Because he is a natural writer, Rand also managed to start up another successful online community — Inbound.org. With a superb online presence, few experts have this kind of influence.

Rand pioneered the development of many SEO tools and has been instrumental in the progression of modern SEO. That was all back in 2004, when the company was still called SEOMoz. In 2014, Rand stepped down as CEO, presumably to spend less time on red tape, and more on SEO. Today, Rand officially serves as an "individual contributor", and he still writes extensively on all sorts of digital topics for the community.

In many ways, Rand was tailoring his company to match Google's search requirements before anyone even knew what they were. With excellent writing and SEO research and a wide variety of big-name contributors adding content to his blog, Moz has become the absolute best industry resource for beginner and intermediate SEO users.

Follow Rand on LinkedIn, Facebook, Google+, Instagram, or on Twitter @randfish.

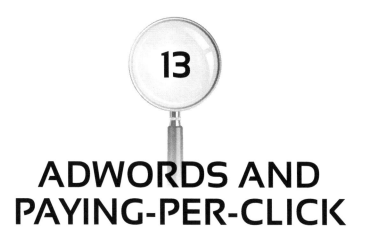

# ADWORDS AND PAYING-PER-CLICK

*"At IMVU, the cost of customer acquisition through our five-dollar-a-day AdWords campaign was less than twenty-five cents. Our revenue from those same customers was more than a dollar."*

Eric Ries, The Lean Startup

If you want to get immediate search engine visibility, there is no better advertising opportunity available today than Google AdWords.[96] Not only is your business easier for people to discover when searching relevant terms on the search engine, but Google makes incredible use of its ad-placement model to encourage clicks for you.

If you can learn how best to bid on your keyword terms and how to customize a Google *pay-per-click* campaign for your website, you can drive hundreds of people to your website simply by targeting specific terms. Best of all, your AdWords campaign can be optimized, i.e., you can make steady improvements as you grow and sell.

---

96 Google AdWords, https://www.google.com/adwords/benefits/

## Your Hidden Keyword Hero

As small business marketers, we love it when a client arrives on our doorstep with an active AdWords campaign that has been running for some time. While 90% of the campaigns that we see underperform, the historical data from a client's existing pay-per-click campaign is priceless.

 If you have been running an AdWords program for any length of time, whether it has been in-house or through an agency, you are sitting on a wealth of information that you can use for search engine optimization.

We have gone through many aspects of the AdWords Keyword Planner Tool in Chapter 6, including search volume averages and other important insights on Google. With a live AdWords program, you can get real user data that is specific to the parameters you set for your own custom program.

There are many ways that you can use AdWords to run tests that will help with your *pay-per-click (PPC)* and SEO campaigns. This is AdWords as you have never seen it — your new keyword hero.

## Using AdWords Alone: The Right Choice?

A great debate continues to rage in the industry regarding how many people click on Google's paid advertisements versus the organic non-paid listings. We speak to *a lot* of small business owners who claim that they personally never click on paid ads. There are statistics, however, that suggest Internet users click on these paid ads around 5% of the time. [97] Others state that users with commercial intent may click on PPC ads around 65% of the time, especially when they are ready to make a purchase. Google and PPC agencies all tend to pump the stats in favor of PPC ads for obvious reasons.

Marketers who specialize in organic SEO promote the benefits of organic rankings over paid advertising for similar reasons. Generally speaking, most accomplished SEO professionals are also great at AdWords, and there is a solid reason for this — training and transparency. With all the certification programs, live phone support, and Google AdWords reps and techs available for ongoing account support, it makes sense.

SEO, on the other hand, is the opposite of transparent, with Google going to extreme lengths to protect its algorithmic secret sauce. SEO experts have to pay very close attention to ranking changes on a daily basis, assess these changes over a period of time, monitor feedback, and test SEO strategies in order to determine what factors get a website to rank. It is vital to find out how those factors are weighted in terms of algorithmic importance. Certified AdWords consultants are a dime a dozen, while true SEO expertise can be significantly harder to find.

Across our stable of clients, we have noticed that about 10-20% of client traffic comes from well-funded, properly optimized AdWords campaigns. That is why we can state with confidence that your company will get five to ten times as much targeted traffic from SEO than from a company that only has a PPC strategy in place with no organic visibility.

Since AdWords is a bid-driven game, some of your competitors may be willing to shave down their profit margins to get those clicks. Google's endgame is, in fact, to make sure that there is no money left on the table in terms of what you are willing to spend on your advertising budget.

---

97  Larry Kim, The War on Free Clicks: Think Nobody Clicks on Google Ads? Think Again!, http://www.wordstream.com/blog/ws/2012/07/17/google-advertising

While AdWords is usually a much better investment than any other form of traditional advertising, it still does not come close to the return on investment from a professionally executed SEO campaign. Great SEO gets you a lot more clicks for a lot less cost per click, period. Low quality, amateur SEO can be a total waste of time or worse, result in a penalty.

## Using SEO and AdWords Combined?

We are not trashing PPC advertising, but nothing can beat top organic Google rankings in terms of ROI. Not social media marketing, not referrals, and not even word of mouth advertising! That does not dismiss the concurrent fact that PPC, specifically AdWords PPC, is the next best thing. Therefore — if it is not clear by now — we strongly suggest that all businesses supplement their organic search engine optimization with a qualified PPC campaign.

The only marketing investment that can beat SEO as a standalone tactic is an SEO campaign that also incorporates an AdWords campaign. This is because, even with the best SEO, it is not possible for a company to rank on the first page of Google for all variations of targeted keyword phrases. You can only cast your organic website net so far. Even if you create new pages with great content, not all of them will automatically rank.

With organic search, your home page and interior pages should rank for their root terms and phrases.[98] AdWords is a fantastic way to pay for clicks on elusive keywords that you or your SEO agency cannot get traction for any other way. With ongoing content marketing, you can use pages on your website and blogs to target other long-tail terms (i.e., keyword phrases) with high conversion potential.

Moreover, since an organic SEO program can take months to get going, you can continue to use your AdWords program to pay for clicks

---

[98] How To Know What Root Keywords Rank Well in Search Engines, http://wpcurve.com/root-keywords/

Google AdWords is also a great way to get immediate search engine visibility while you setup your website and SEO and ramp up your content marketing efforts.

until those rankings improve. Then you can adjust your PPC strategy according to the performance of your organic rankings.

Over time, you will build up AdWords tracking data, which becomes invaluable for SEO. Your organic and PPC strategy only get better once you have reviewed and applied this data to those campaigns.

Four More Reasons to Use AdWords for SEO Right Now

As you have discovered, the combined force of SEO and PPC can be a magical thing for your website traffic. Beyond the obvious, there are four additional reasons why you should use AdWords in conjunction with a competent organic SEO campaign.

## Reason #1: Proof of Concept Testing

In recent years we have been using AdWords as a proof-of-concept strategy for our clients. We build a simple, but effective, landing page and fund an AdWords campaign for a month or two. If the landing page generates qualified leads and has sales conversions, then it becomes fantastic evidence that investing in a long term SEO strategy is logical next step.

## Reason #2: Conversion Testing

One of our favorite SEO ninja tactics is to spend time creating and installing conversion-tracking code in all the right places. This includes tracking which keywords trigger a contact email message, and which keyword clicks result in phone calls to your business.

Most websites do not use conversion tracking! Of the websites that do, few use dynamic phone conversion tracking, which is an awesome AdWords feature. Once you have your conversion data tied to specific keywords, you have the proverbial bull's eye and can target your top keywords for SEO success.

### Reason #3: Click-Through Rate (CTR) Testing

AdWords gives you the chance to manipulate the main ad title (blue title text) and the descriptive text in your ad. You can experiment with ad copy to optimize your text ads' click-through rate (CTR). CTR is thought by many to be a major ranking factor in organic search, so your AdWords testing in live ads can further optimize the page title and meta descriptions on your web pages. Higher organic click through rates correlate to higher ranking results on Google.

### Reason #4: Call to Action Testing

AdWords may be the best way to test the call-to-action (CTA) triggers on your website. [99] For example, we like to offer free eBooks on our websites, many of which are available at:

**http://DuctTapePublishing.com**

With AdWords, we can test eBook giveaways with PPC ads to see which eBooks convert better than others, then pick the one that gets the most sign ups. Getting the right CTA on your website will make the difference between a good SEO campaign and a great one.

## How to Use AdWords to Crush Your Competition

Pay-per-click advertising is a great way to hit your competition quickly and where it hurts — in their market share. The beauty of AdWords is that you can immediately get search engine visibility for the best

---

[99] Nick Eppinger, Essential Guide To Testing AdWords Ad Copy – Part 1, http://www. lunametrics.com/blog/2015/08/03/adwords-testing-guide-part-1/

Co-Author Phil Singleton has developed a WordPress plugin for installing AdWords tracking code on individual pages and posts, along with sitewide use. With this free plugin, you can easily insert AdWords tracking code on your individual posts and pages for data collection!

**https://wordpress.org/plugins/adwords-conversion-tracking-code/**

keyword searches, and you are guaranteed to get the top spot if you pay for it.

When targeting the competition, there are a few things that you need to keep in mind when it comes to copyright and trademark concerns. You cannot use your competitor's name in your ad copy, for one. This is likely to violate AdWords policy. [100] We suggest you read this policy from start to finish and follow the guidelines closely.

While you cannot put your competitor's name in your ad copy without their permission, you can bid on their trademark as a keyword in your PPC campaign. This means that when people search for your competitor's name and variations of it, your ad will appear at the top of those searches. This is an excellent way to leverage your competitor's marketing dollar, especially if you know that they have invested heavily in TV, print, and radio advertising.

---

100 AdWords Trademark Policy, https://support.google.com/adwordspolicy/answer/6118?hl=en

There are some amazing third- party services like SEMRush.com that will provide you with very specific information about your competitors' AdWords program, cost-per-click data, and insight into what your competitors are spending now. If you want to know how their PPC budget has changed over time, use these important SEO tools.

Traditional advertising inevitably attracts people to the Internet, when they search for contact information, reviews, and other information on your competitors. You can take advantage of your competitors' expensive demand-creation advertising and snatch away their sales as they filter through the online sales funnel.

## Getting Started With AdWords

Account setup is straightforward and easy, but optimizing it can be tricky. Keep in mind that AdWords is the sole reason why Google exists, and why it is worth hundreds of billions of dollars. The system is rigged to get you to spend as much of your advertising budget as possible.

When you initially setup a Google AdWords account, [101] Google guides you to overspend— so it is up to you to refine your AdWords campaign to get the best return on your investment. In recent years, Google has increased support for AdWords and now has live phone support. It may even assign personal AdWords account reps to your business.

That said, most advice that you get from your Google support team will likely steer you toward increasing your PPC budget. AdWords

---

101 Ready To Get Started?, https://www.google.com/adwords/get-started/

expert Perry Marshall uses an exceptional analogy to describe taking AdWords support advice; he says that it is akin to letting a German Shepherd guard ham sandwiches. A less glamorous analogy might be that of a drug addict asking a drug dealer how much money she should spend on drugs. Either way, the point comes through loud and clear. Consider who is giving you AdWords advice and where you are finding it, and take what they say with a grain of salt if there is a clear conflict of interest.

The AdWords control panel is intimidating in terms of all the setup options, research tools, and data tracking tools. This system is constantly being updated. There are entire books written about AdWords, because it is so broad and extensive to use.

Consider hiring a professional to deal with this for you. Of course, you do not have to hire anyone at all. AdWords is set up specifically for DIY use, and any agency you hire would be using the same control panel to set up and manage your ad campaigns.

AdWords is one aspect of online marketing where it may be worth your investment to hire a professional to help you setup an account. We would recommend considering a qualified agency for a long-term partnership.

## Top Ten AdWords Setup Tips for Business Owners

There are so many superb features in AdWords, it can be hard to name them all or even scratch the surface of its vast functionality. Some features allow you to adjust your budget for mobile clicks and improve conversion rates and features. The dynamic keyword insertion function for ad template creation, for example, allows you to automatically insert keywords into your PPC ad.

We could cover hundreds of features in AdWords and still have to add the dozens more that were added while this book was being published. Or we could do something more practical and give you some basic tips that will help save your business hundreds, even thousands, of dollars on your first AdWords campaign. Here they are:

1. Always select your geographic territory so that your ads are only shown to people in that physical location. You can choose by state, metro area, zip code, or country, among many other options.

2. Always select "people in your targeted location" and NOT "people in, searching for, or who show interest in your targeted location" — if you only want clicks from people physically located in your market area. Otherwise, you may get clicks from people located in other states or even other countries.

3. Pay careful attention to the keyword phrases that you choose,[102] and take note that AdWords defaults to "broad matches," so you may want to refine this to "phrase matches" or even "exact matches" for greater accuracy and clearer tracking data.

4. Use the "negative keywords" feature in your ad campaigns so that you don't get people looking for non-buy words like "free" or "cheap" or "jobs." Otherwise you will waste precious marketing dollars serving your ads to people not interested in buying from you.

5. Setup conversion tracking for clicks that result in both phone calls and emails.

6. Use the free ad extensions so that you can show more information in your PPC ads (usually only shown when your bid amount is high enough to get you ranked among the top four PPC results).

---

102 Using Keyword Matching Options, **https://support.google.com/adwords/answer/2497836?hl=en**

Add your phone number, sitelinks for more direct links to other pages on your website, and callouts for more ad copy text in your PPC ad.

7. Link your account to your Google My Business page so that Google can pull in more data for your ads — for free. This gives you some of the best data you can get, in terms of exact phrasing that a user typed in, and what you paid for that click.

8. In each ad group, monitor the keyword terms in the 'dimensions' tab. This is the only way to view the exact terms people searched when they got, and clicked on, your PPC ad.

9. Use the retargeting feature in AdWords, which will allow you to set up *graphic display ads* that follow users on third-party websites. This is a great feature, though it can take some time to set up.

10. Finally, do not be afraid to set up a healthy initial budget for a month or two, with the knowledge that it can later be refined for a greater ROI. If you set the initial budget too small, you are unlikely to get the information you need to improve, and you will not see the real potential of a refined PPC campaign.

## Experts to Watch: *Perry Marshall*[103]

Perry Marshall is a well-known AdWords pioneer, having devised many of the best practices in the industry since AdWords became a product worth using. He is best known for his book on Internet advertising, *The Ultimate Guide to Google AdWords*.

Perry is a strong advocate for split testing and online advertising, and he teaches his followers how the 80/20 rule is the central strategy he uses for all of his sales, business, and marketing practices. His book, *80/20 Sales & Marketing*, continues to be among the best available to companies today.

---

103 About Perry Marshall, https://www.perrymarshall.com/bio/

Aside from these pillars of marketing wisdom, Perry has also written several other books, including *The Ultimate Guide to Facebook Advertising*, *Industrial Ethernet*, and *Evolution 2.0: Breaking the Deadlock Between Darwin and Design* — all of which are bestselling titles. Has also been cited in dozens of modern influential texts and books by many of the top content marketing names of today.

Perry continues to be a stand-out influencer if you want to learn about PPC. He offers a number of interesting products for sale on his website that can educate you on the inner workings of Google's AdWords platform. We strongly recommend you sign up for his email list and investigate his other educational content pieces.

# GOOGLE ANALYTICS AND SEARCH CONSOLE

*"Without big data analytics, companies are blind and deaf, wandering out onto the Web like deer on a freeway."*

Geoffrey Moore, Best Selling Author

There are three fundamental ways to get essential data from Google: *AdWords*, *Google Analytics*, and *Google Search Console*. Each of these SEO pillars provides you with a wealth of knowledge that can be analyzed, interpreted, and used to inform an effective SEO strategy. We have already covered the AdWords Keyword Planner in detail, so this chapter will focus on Google Analytics and Google Search Console.

Google Analytics (GA) is a tool that you can use to better understand your traffic and the behavior of your users while they are on your website.[104] Along with the other tools mentioned in previous chapters,

---

104 The Importance of Clean and Meaningful Google Analytics Data, http://www.analytics-ninja.com/blog/2013/02/getting-clean-and-meaningful-google-analytics-data.html

it can help you reverse engineer a perfectly optimized website from the ground up. Launching an SEO-friendly website is only half the game. You will also need to continually monitor your traffic and the health of your website, tweaking it for SEO indefinitely.

The key to succeeding in the new era of content-driven SEO is to understand how users search, where they come from, who they are, and how they interact with you on your website and with your content. When you consistently monitor your website performance, you will get a better idea about which strategies work and which do not work.

Understanding your website traffic is not just about SEO. You can also use this information to track and measure how your traditional marketing efforts are doing. For example, many advertising campaigns include a special-purpose landing page. But even marketing and advertising that does not point directly back to your website can result in visits.

Getting information on a traffic spike and your user data can help you refine and measure your ROI so that you can better manage your efforts. All roads in this book lead back to great content. It is your ability to use GA data to find and create great content which will set you apart from other companies.

The ability to look back at traffic, your user base, and where it is coming from allows you to create better, more targeted content for these individuals. With this data, content ideas are based on conversion instead of whim. You can also find sites that link to you, and use this referral tracking information to form new partnerships or create content distribution opportunities that you did not know existed.

## The Exponential Power of Google Analytics

It is difficult to cover all of the features and benefits of GA here, because there are so many. There are entire books and educational training programs dedicated to teaching people how to use and interpret GA data. The only problem with GA is the abundance of information.

There are more ways to slice up and analyze the traffic on your website than there is information on your site. But there is exponential power in using GA to guide your SEO and other online marketing strategies for your website.

The traffic and user data GA provides can solve your website's content problems as they arise. You can also use it to regularly improve your content, through trial and error and test campaigns. And the insights you generate from GA data can lead to new goals, strategies, and tactics. You get a huge competitive edge when you focus on evidence-based SEO and content creation for your website.

## Free Training and Certification

Google is known for developing incredible tools that anyone can use for free to improve their website performance. The problem is that these tools can be tricky to use, and they take some in-depth study. The good news is that Google understands that, and, in the spirit of helping business owners and others learn how to use GA properly, it developed a training and certification program that anyone can take for free.[105]

**QUICK TIP**

In order to get a handle on Google Analytics we strongly advise you to take advantage of Google's free certification program. It will train you for free on how to get the most out of their tools, and on how to draw quality insights from this data for better content development.

---

105 Google Analytics Training & Certification, http://www.google.com/analytics/learn/index.html

The training program was developed to help users learn how to analyze their data. So to get started, all you have to do is run through the setup checklist and have a GA account that is linked to a website address.

The course comes in multimedia format; there are videos, resource pages, and practice activities that you can use to brush up on your GA processes. Enjoy using Google's study guide system, which has comprehensive notes on each GA area. Once you have used the Analytics Academy to orient yourself in your data, you can choose to do the GA Individual Qualification test.

If you pass, you will receive an official industry-recognized qualification from Google at no cost. We believe that all web designers should have this qualification, and some business owners should consider taking this test too. It does a lot to get you oriented in the new movement of data analysis sweeping through the online marketing world right now.

Google also offers you the chance to deepen your knowledge by attending scheduled GA training classes taught by one of its certified partners. You can do a 101 course, an intermediate course, or you can even go for the advanced course. There are many videos and other resources on YouTube that Google offers as well.

With this qualification, you will be fully versed in how to use this amazing tool to improve your website performance, sales, and online marketing.

## The Amazing Benefits of Tracking and Analysis

Setting up a GA account is free and easy. Even installing the tracking code script is straightforward, though it may be beyond the comfort level of many business owners. If you have a WordPress website, plugins make this super fast.

If you are comfortable with WordPress, you can also install the script right in your header.php file, under the <body> tag. Or send the script to your web designer who can install it for you in seconds. Either way, there are some amazing benefits of using tracking and analysis for your business online. Beyond simple website insights, GA is an essential marketing and strategic tool that can help your business grow online.

On the whole, GA provides you with four main business benefits. [106] The first of these is marketing campaign optimization. All online marketing campaigns should be tracked and measured so that they can be optimized and improved upon during the next campaign cycle. GA gives you a way to measure if your strategies are working or not.[107]

Benchmarking your previous marketing campaign results and then tweaking the campaign accordingly allows you to assess whether or not those content changes were beneficial to your conversion goals or whether they actually had a negative impact on your results. Ongoing marketing optimization is the key to streamlining your website online for bigger, better sales.

**QUICK TIP** Content marketers use Google Analytics when developing website content. They will usually create two or more pages, then test how that content performs by splitting the incoming traffic and assessing the impact of the content. This is called **A/B testing** or **split testing**. If the goal is conversion, one page will always perform better than another. This is how optimized landing pages and website pages are created from data.

---

106 Gemma Holloway, The Business Benefits of Google Analytics, http://www.koozai.com/blog/analytics/google-analytics-business-benefits/

107 How To Do A/B Split Testing in WordPress Using Google Analytics, http://www.wpbeginner.com/wp-tutorials/how-to-ab-split-testing-in-wordpress-using-google-analytics/

The second business benefit involves website usability improvement. Through close interpretation of the data, you can determine what kind of content works best with your specific target demographic. With in-depth content analysis, you can break down exactly what content your user base wants and how you can best provide it to them.

GA's Behavior and Conversion Reports sections are all about user satisfaction, and they give you lots of information on how it can be improved. Which pages most engage your users? Which pages get users to linger? Which pages cause your users to click, act, or buy?

Audience Reports are provide great insight into which devices people are using to access your website.

Target audience identification is a third business benefit, which helps you streamline not only your website, but your business model too. Information such as user age, gender, and interests can all be used to develop stronger content and campaigns.

Finally, GA assists with budget allocations. Based on the insight derived from your data, you will be able to determine what sort of financial investment is needed to improve things to a level that gets you the right conversion. This is excellent for ROI and budget efficiency, which can become a major issue in online marketing.

## The Data you can get From Google Analytics

GA offers a lot of data you can use on your quest to improve your website content and design. What you do with this data determines your online success. Here is the kind of data Google Analytics offers you for insight deduction:

### Your Core Visitor Data

There is a lot of data available in this area, but the following metrics have been found to be the most important.

- **Total Visits**: Total number of user visits over a specific period of time (includes repeat visits)

- *Unique Visits*: Total number of unique visits (not including repeat visits)
- *Page Views*: How many website pages were viewed
- *Pages Per Visit*: How many web pages were viewed by a user during a unique visit
- *Average Visit Duration*: How long a user stays on your website in a given visit
- *Percentage of New Visitors*: The number of new visitors on your website relative to the total number of visitors for a given date range
- *Bounce Rate*: The percentage of single-page sessions,[108] or visitors who leave a website after arriving on the landing page instead of viewing more pages

In web analytics, a high **bounce rate** suggests that the content on the page is not entirely relevant to the user, especially when the user leaves quickly. Lowering your bounce rate on key pages by making the content more relevant can keep people in your **sales conversion cycle** for longer, which can improve sales, or at the very least, encourage more page views.

## How Your Visitors Found You

- *Organic Search*: *Organic traffic* derived from Google Search results

---

108 Bounce Rate, https://support.google.com/analytics/answer/1009409?hl=en

- *AdWords*: You can link your AdWords account to your Analytics account and view traffic data from PPC campaigns
- *Referrals*: Traffic from third-party sources, like someone clicking on a link to your blog on someone else's website
- *Social Networks*: Social media networks like Facebook, Instagram, and Twitter
- *Direct Traffic*: Users directly typing in your web address into the browser
- *Audience Demographics and Insights*
- *Age and Gender*: Your users' age and gender data
- *Interests:* Their interests, such as technology, sports and cooking
- *Location*: Where they users live (country, state, and city)
- *Technology:* What technology they use (browser, operating system, Internet provider)
- *User Flow*: How people enter your site and the page paths they took to exiting your site

Real-Time Data is incredibly useful as well, because you can see live user data on your website that shows off many of the above- mentioned insights in real-time charts and graphs. Keyword information is also available, though not as extensively as it once was.

At one time, you were able to see how users came to your site from Google Search by the keyword they used. But everything changed in 2011 when Google moved to https.[109] Remember **SSL**, the encryption protocol that Google wants everyone to have?

Google is also concerned with protecting personalized search activity, which is why it now encrypts all search queries. Google's rationale is that if a user connects to Google Search via **SSL**, then that user has an expectation of security, and Google should not share this personal information with third parties (such as website owners). Thus, they have

---

109 Evelyn Kao, Making Search More Secure, http://googleblog.blogspot.com/2011/10/making-search-more-secure.html

removed a lot of keyword tracking data from Google Analytics, thereby hiding a lot of useful data for search engine optimization. The ability to know exactly which keyword phrases users clicked on through organic search was very powerful. Now, instead of seeing detailed keyword data in Google Analytics, you are more likely to see an entry titled "not provided."

There are some advanced level hacks that you can use to harvest organic keyword data, but none are as comprehensive or as easy as they once were in GA. Google will still provide you with exact keyword and search phrase data in AdWords, however, because you are paying for it.

## Google Search Console (formerly Webmaster Tools)

Google Webmaster Tools recently changed its name and has been redubbed Google Search Console. You can manage several websites from your dashboard and invite third parties to access the information as well, which is very useful if you have a SEO expert or webmaster on staff.

Google Search Console (GSC)[110] is Google's free service that helps you track, monitor, and maintain your website's presence in its search results. Using Google's tools, you can optimize each process for greater success.

GSC has seven major areas, along with the famous dashboard area.

Here is a rundown on each of them:

### Search Appearance Section

This tool will help you audit some of your website's SEO coding attributes. You can give Google specific instructions about the intent behind certain content areas on your web pages, and you can find opportunities to improve your on-page SEO.

- *Structured data:* Remember website coding and schema? In this section, GSC gives you insight into your structured data.

---

110 What Is Search Console, https://support.google.com/webmasters/answer/4559176?hl=en

- *Data highlighter:* This is a powerful little tool. It allows you to create a Google-structured data template for your webpages, so that you do not have to create and install special SEO markup code on your website. You simply pull up a page on your website and highlight and tag content. A product page, for example, can be selected as a product page template, and you can tag sections without having to go into the code on your website. This is great for price, image, name, votes, star ratings, reviews, and reviewer details.

## HTML Improvements

It is a best practice to have unique titles and meta-descriptions on your home page, inner pages, and in your blog posts. Your GSC account will show you how many pages have duplicate meta-descriptions and non-indexable content.

### Search Traffic Section

*Search Analytics:* There is some overlap between AdWords, Google Analytics, and Google Search Console. One area is with search traffic, though GSC allows you to see it through a different lens. Here you can see clicks and keyword data from the last 90 days. *Impressions* — the number of times a web page comes up on a search result page that was viewed by a user — are our favorite. This is awesome information for SEO campaigns. Seeing rising *impressions* is a good sign, even if your clicks have not yet risen; that will happen when your site starts to appear on the second page or the bottom of the first page.

- *External Links To Your Site:* Potentially the most important tool in GSC. In this area, you can see all the links that Google is counting towards your website. No other third-party tool gives you better data on this. Review these links, and use the information to take action or reduce your Penguin penalty risk. Here you can also learn how people link to your website, whether it be through raw links, generic "more info" links, or *keyword phrase anchor links.*

- *Internal Links Within Your Site:* Internal or *page-to-page linking* within your own website can be seen here. This is an important ranking factor to get right, and there are on-page ranking risks courtesy of Panda that you need to check. Here is where you can see how many links you have on each page, and which pages they are coming from.

- *Manual Actions:* As we discussed earlier, Google sometimes takes manual actions against offending sites. Here you will find a list of these actions and links to steps that you can take to sort out any offending concerns.

- *Mobile Usability:* If your website has issues related to mobile users, you will receive messages from Google about them here.

## Google Index Section

- *Index Status:* Here you will receive reports on URLs that Google has indexed in relation to your website. These include total-indexed URLs, and URLs that have been blocked or removed.

- *Content Keywords:* This is where you will find the keyword lists and their variants that Google discovered while crawling your website. Unexpected keywords can mean that your website has been hacked.

- *Blocked Resources:* [111] This report helps you discover images, CSS, and Javascript that Googlebot crawler cannot reach because they are somehow blocked. The Fetch and Render tool shows you how Google sees your web page.

- *Remove URL:* You can use Google's temporary URL-blocking tool to address urgent content changes that need immediate action in the search results.

---

111 Barry Schwartz, Google Webmaster Toosl Adds Blocked Resources Report & Updates Fetch & Render Tool, http://searchengineland.com/google-webmaster-tools-adds-blocked-resources-report-updates-fetch-render-tool-216558

## Crawl Section

- *Google Crawling:* How Google gathers and organizes information from your website so it can index your content and rank you.
- *Googlebot:* Google's web crawling bot, also called a spider. This is how Google discovers new and updated web pages online.
- *Crawl Stats:* This page gives you information on Googlebot's activity on your website for the past 90 days.
- *Crawl Errors:* This report gives you details about the site URLs that Google could not successfully crawl or that returned an error code.
- *Fetch as Google:* A tool that you can use to test how Google crawls your website.
- *Robots.txt Tester: A robots.txt file* is a file at the root of your website that tells Google which parts of your site you do not want accessed by its *search engine crawlers.* This is one of those professional sections that require an SEO expert.
- *Sitemaps:* [112] An SEO sitemap is a model of a website's content to help search engine crawlers and users navigate the website. This is where your website sitemap will go, which informs Google about the organization of your site content.
- *Security:* The security issues section — not surprisingly — is where Google communicates with you about any security issues such as site hacks, malware, and other malicious code.

## Growing Sales and Commerce

Using Google Search Console in conjunction with Google Analytics is a superb way to grow your website sales and expand commerce online. With every sectional report, you will be given a host of information that you will have to then convert into usable insights.

---

112 Site Map, Techopedia, http://www.techopedia.com/definition/5393/site-map

Google Search Console is easy to set up and verify. Set up your Google Analytics account first, and then you will be given an option to verify your GSC account with your verified GA tracking script already installed on your website. It's one-click verification from there.

That means developing a method of assessing or analyzing the data to derive insights and converting those into concrete marketing or content action. With evidence-based website content and marketing practices, you will find that the sales on your website rapidly grow.

Use these reports to improve your SEO and ramp up your content offering to encourage higher conversions on your chosen sales web pages. Using GSC and content split testing, you can improve conversion rates for each page to optimize the traffic you get, and substantially increase your chances that this traffic becomes a sale. Once you have established reliable conversion rates on your actionable web pages, your marketing budget will become easier to apply.

All it takes is some basic knowledge of Google Search Console and Analytics and figuring how to best use the data these tools provide in your ongoing content, SEO, and online marketing pursuits. The companies that grow the fastest in the future will be the ones tapping into this rich data source.

## Expert to Watch: *Glenn Gabe*[113]

Glenn Gabe is one of the most intelligent minds in technical SEO in the world today. He is an established and highly successful digital marketing consultant at G-Squared Interactive, with a specialized focus on SEO,

---

113 About Glenn Gabe, http://www.gsqi.com/about-glenn-gabe/

SEM, social advertising, and website analytics.

For more than two decades years, Glenn has led teams in the field of search engine optimization, helping clients across a wide range of industries discover the power of evidence-based marketing. Glenn also writes incredibly detailed posts for top online tech sites such as Search Engine Land.

He is the author of a popular blog on Internet marketing, called The Internet Marketing Driver, where he has a large community of dedicated followers. He uses his blog as a content source to fuel his company, G-Squared Interactive. He has also written for the official Bing Ads Blog and was a featured author in the Google Analytics Help Center.

If you are looking for a leader who understands how to convert data insights into sales, then following Glenn on Twitter @glenngabe and Google+ and subscribing to his blog is an excellent idea.

# FEEDING YOUR OPTIMIZED WEBSITE

*"It is not the job of search engine optimization to make a pig fly. It is the job of the SEO [professional] to genetically reengineer the website so that it becomes an eagle."*

Bruce Clay, Bruce Clay, Inc.

## The Tools you Need to Dominate

All SEO experts have their favorite tools. Here is a list of the tools and platforms we love the most:

**WordPress** (for informational websites and e-commerce sites)

- Function: An open source content management system that helps you manage your website content without any formal training
- Value: Ability to edit website, upload content, and optimize for on-page SEO

### Magento (for large scale e-commerce websites)

- Function: E-commerce software that makes selling online easier
- Value: Well-supported, SEO-friendly e-commerce solution for larger businesses

### Yoast SEO

- Function: Comprehensive WordPress plugin which helps you optimize your website and content for search engines
- Value: With the right strategy, it helps fully optimize your website sitewide and page-by-page

### WordPress SEO Structured Data Schema

- Function: Easily add JSON-LD *structured data markup* to your WordPress website
- Value: Your web pages have a better chance of generating *rich snippets* directly in search results such as star ratings, event details, customer reviews, and more

### Sucuri.net

- Function: Protects websites from hacks, malware, and spam
- Value: Content safety, black hat SEO flagging, real-time monitoring, website firewall protection, and malware removal support

### BlogVault.com

- Function: Backs up your WordPress website on a third-party location for security and migration purposes
- Value: Daily site backups, ability to recover your website instantly from hacks or user error with one-click site restores

### UpCity.com

- Function: Local inbound marketing platform for digital agencies and businesses
- Value: All-in-one SEO task management, keyword rank tracking, local SEO, reputation management, and social content marketing

## Ahrefs.com

- Function: SEO backlink research analysis tool
- Value: Monitor and assess backlink opportunities for your own website's off-page SEO and for competing websites

## SEMRush.com

- Function: Discover important competition data for SEO and content research
- Value: Improve your SEO and content while reverse engineering your competition's for both organic search and paid search

## ExpressWriters.com

- Function: On-demand content created by a large pool of talented writers
- Value: Access high-quality, custom content whenever you need it, at a set price

## BuzzSumo.com

- Function: Tracks and ranks content that performs best on sites such as Facebook, Twitter, LinkedIn, Google+, and Pinterest
- Value: Discover top content that is trending *right now*, find influencers for outreach, blogging topics, and guest blogging opportunities

## Emphatic.co

- Function: Social media management service
- Value: Curates articles based on your guidelines, handwrites commentary, and posts to your social media accounts for you

## Grade.us

- Function: Online reputation management
- Value: Automated customer review funnel to easily manage, monitor, collect, and display more positive reviews online

### eReleases.com

- Function: Online press release distribution service that is affordable and effective
- Value: Gets your press release on PR Newswire, syndication by hundreds of news and media websites, and email distribution to over 100,000 subscribing journalists and bloggers

### Moz Local

- Function: Local business listing management
- Value: Creates and maintains business listings on the sites, apps, and directories that factor most into local search engine results

### Copyscape.com

- Function: Online plagiarism detection service
- Value: Ensures your content is original and helps you avoid duplicate content penalties from Google and other search engines

### SocialQuant.net

- Function: Helps you build targeted Twitter followers
- Value: Increases your social media reach organically and leads to increased engagement with your content

### *Google Tools:*

### Search Console (Formerly Webmaster Tools)114

- Function: Helps you see your website through Google's eyes
- Value: Streamlines how Google crawls, analyzes, and indexes your website

### AdWords Keyword Planner

- Function: Discover the right keywords to use in SEO campaigns
- Value: Get more targeted customers and find hidden micro-niches for traffic, and maybe even discover new business opportunities

---

114 Kevin Vertommen, Everything You Need To Know About Google Search Console, http://webdesign.tutsplus.com/articles/everything-you-need-to-know-about-google-search-console--cms-24069

### Google Analytics

- Function: Track, analyze, and monitor your website's traffic
- Value: Improve your performance across all channels for increased sales

### Structured Data Tool (within Google Search Console)

- Function: Helps Google understand what your content is a about
- Value: Increases the chance that more information about your content will be displayed in search results, such as start ratings, event times, etc.

### Mobile-Friendly Test

- Function: Test whether your website is mobile-friendly
- Value: Identify issues with your site in mobile device view so you can fix and meet Google's mobile mobile-friendliness guidelines

## Content Generation Hacks

Content is the heart of your online lead generation system. Creating excellent posts for your website blog, for example, can be a time-consuming and tedious process for a small business with limited staff and resources. You need to know some time-saving content generation hacks to keep your content machine fed.

You can do this using an inbound strategy. The planning and analysis of historical data can help you gain an understanding of what people have been searching for in your niche. Then you can use social engagement tools to see what is trending online today. With this strategy, you can weave keyword targets into highly sharable content that will generate the coveted social signals you need to rank well, and quickly.

Catching these content waves is just one method of employing real-time SEO to gain search engine visibility. A very big part of this process involves building a sustainable content machine, so that you always have access to fresh content when you need it.

A few more content generation hacks involve leveraging this content generation machine with SEO. [115] Create list posts about industry experts, tips, or tricks, and integrate quality keywords into these posts. People love to read them because they are practical, and they are shared for the same reasons.

How-to posts are *always* in demand. You can also use content to teach your audience how to do something it could not do before. People want to DIY things from the comfort of their PC screens these days. If you can help them out with an educational post containing your target keywords, great.

In order to succeed at content-driven SEO, you need to be able to complete a long list of initial setup and ongoing SEO tasks to achieve and maintain organic search engine rankings. We highly recommend **UpCity.com**, the leading local inbound marketing platform for small businesses. No other solution on the market does a better job of managing social media, reputation, and SEO tasks, in addition to providing automated reporting.

You should also include content that naturally answers customers' questions. Referred to as "answer FAQs," these tend to rank well over time. Create a list of common questions and answers, then convert these into hard-hitting and highly entertaining posts. You should also curate content, and add in your opinion or provide your brand's spin on it to make it special.

---

115 Anum Hussain, 15 Insider Tips For Creating a Content Creation Machine, http://blog. hubspot.com/marketing/tips-to-build-a-marketing-content-machine

Remarkable content can be reworked into new posts, or commented on by someone on your team. Always take advantage of content that makes use of data, because it tends to be shared more often. Statistics and case study posts have a very far reach on social media.

Don't forget to create evergreen content for your website and to update any historical content on your site that might be outdated, lest it lose SEO value. All your live online content should be current and there for SEO reasons.

## Content Curation Insight

There is one practice which many expert content marketers use to plug the gaps in their content machine. It is called "content curation insight," and it basically involves curating content on a given topic and adding an authority's opinion. All it takes is finding and reading the content on a given topic in a niche, summarizing each piece in 2-3 lines, and adding in an opinion. These pieces of content can be transformed into any format: video, text, image, or otherwise.

This technique is so powerful because readers want to know from a trusted source if something is worth reading. As industries broaden, and dozens of experts on a single topic begin to generate closed content loops with large volumes of SEO content, people become disinterested in the information. Instead, they look for a person or figurehead to help them make sense of things. A small business owner can therefore become a niche influencer just by curating the most important content in her niche for her communities.

Crafting these brief summations creates the opportunity to grow your audience, especially if your opinions are useful for your reader. As time goes by, your name will become synonymous with other leaders in your field, all because of this brief, effective content marketing technique.

Websites like Scoop.it have pioneered this form of content creation, and sites like it have sparked a generation of influencers and opinion leaders. These posts can even take the form of several curated pieces of content or links with an assessment attached to each.

Creating 10+ content curation insight posts every month is hugely beneficial to your SEO strategy, especially if you tag the expert on whom you are offering insight. Everything from eBooks, blog posts, whitepapers, and slideshows can be curated and used in your campaign. If it helps your customer, tell them how, and sum it up for them in laymen's terms.

If you are providing your readers with a service, they will choose to follow your account instead of — or at least in addition to — competing sources. In a crowded content marketplace, the strongest, most entertaining voices are the ones that gain the largest followings. Community size, as you know, is a big plus for your SEO strategy.

Adding meaning or a fresh perspective on older or "hot" content is a great way to get noticed by different people on different networks. These posts can attract leads that filter over to your website as people begin to see you as a thought leader.

There are five main types of content curation that you can take advantage of for SEO: [116]

1. ***Elevation*** → providing insight on a batch of posts
2. ***Aggregation*** → collecting and synthesizing content into one post
3. ***Distillation*** → building original content from that written by many voices

---

[116] Jayson DeMers, Your Guide To Content Curation For SEO, http://www. searchenginejournal.com/guide-content-curation-seo/80773/

4. *Chronology* → using a historical timeline to organize content

5. *Mashups* → combining different content for a fresh perspective

## Creating a Closed-Circle Content Loop (Feeding the Content Monster)

If there is one thing Google loves more than anything, it is fresh content. Its algorithms are getting better and better at finding and ranking the best content online. As we have detailed, backlinks, once the most heavily weighted signal, have become just another ranking factor. If you're going to have any real shot at competing in this new SEO era, you must be dedicated to creating and distributing high-quality content, which will generate genuine social signals. As they say, content is king.

Text content in the form of articles and blog posts is key, but you also need to consider creating other types of content for distribution. *Podcasts*, presentations, infographics, photos, eBooks, and videos are important to generating a diverse content offering. All of these content areas will help you build a content machine that improves your SEO.

**QUICK TIP** A *closed-circle content loop* is an inbound content system you create for your company, in which many different types of content are generated and old content is recycled and reused in new, relevant ways. This is an effective strategy for maintaining a constant stream of fresh content for your brand online.

Content creation is a necessary ongoing investment. [117] This means taking the time to create it or spending money on having another writer create it for you. Either way, you need a constant supply of content to feed your inbound marketing machine. Repurposing content is one strategy you can use to cut down on the time and costs of creating fresh content.

When you can reuse content, and you have a system that helps you do this when the time is right, you will save money in the long run. To achieve this, consider what can be done with repurposed content:

- Create a content calendar that resembles the table of contents for a book, or a user guide, or a blog series. Decide when your content will be outdated and in need of repurposing and mark it on the calendar.

- Start creating and publishing each post as a series on your blog. Use each post to create a companion podcast series. At the end of the series, compile your blog posts into an eBook to use as a call-to-action carrot on your website.

To feed the content monster, no one piece of content that you create should ever remain as is or be allowed to stagnate or outdate. By keeping track of your content publication dates in an Excel spreadsheet and setting a date for repurposing them, you will be able to use one piece of content many times.

Old social media posts can be repurposed into eBooks for your fans. An image series can be used in your next slideshow. Blog posts can become videos. One piece of content can always become something fresh if published in a new format. And that means fresh content for Google, which — as we've repeatedly noted — loves this most of all.

---

117 Sujan Patel, 37+ Tips and Resources For Building a Fine-Tuned Content Marketing Machine From The Ground Up, https://blog.bufferapp.com/37-tips-resources-building-fine-tuned-content-marketing-machine-ground

## Ten Best Practices for Content Creation

Here are our ten best tips for content creation, which should help you create more effective content for your new inbound marketing machine.

**#1: Quality matters, but so does quantity**. Just because Google demands quality content now, does not mean you can get away with publishing one blog post a month. Unfortunately, if you still want to see real SEO results, you have to publish higher volumes of quality content too. For most small businesses, that means at least two to four times per month.

**#2: Titles are the most important**. We live in the Internet age when most of what is read is a title in passing. That makes your post titles the most important content you will create. Use them to grab attention, attract readers, clicks, and new fans. If you can get them with your headline, they will read your posts.

**#3: Keywords belong in all content**. From your titles to your body text, captions, and video descriptions, all of your content needs to contain the right keywords for SEO.[118] There is real power in building up a solid base of SEO content online. Your traffic numbers will explode, and you will have many assets to repurpose.

**#4: Content must convert**. Content is not created just to attract readers and crawlers. It also has to convert your readers into paying customers. If this is your goal, you will need to explore the world of writing persuasive copy for different media. Words convert better than any other form of content online.

**#5: Have a content strategy**. Your individual pieces of content should also make sense as a collection. You will be creating many different types of content for SEO, and each of these must be part of an ongoing content strategy. Otherwise you will never be able to snag conversions with lazy topics and poorly conceived themes.

---

118 Mike Murray, 4 Online Content Best Practices For Success, http://contentmarketinginstitute.com/2014/01/online-content-best-practices-for-2014/

**#6: Create resource lists.** All SEO savvy content creators have favorite websites, influencers, and content sources that they trust. These are the places where you find the best information to use for your own content. Keep a list, and add or remove content locations as needed. This list will become a key asset in your content system.

**#7: Curate as well as create.** Content can be created from scratch (no resources used), or you can create something original that is inspired by other people's content. You can also curate other content from different places. This will help keep you going and prevent you from wasting too much time creating long pieces of original content.

**#8: If you want variation, get different writers.** Different voices can be a major pull for a blog or social media page. It adds a fresh dynamic to your brand and invites fans and customers to engage with your team.

**#9: Invite your community to become content creators.** This one is straightforward. Given the chance, some of your community members will be glad to create educational posts for you to gain exposure and build their own authority.

**#10: Track and analyze all content performance**. If you want to know what content works for your brand, track it. You can analyze the data and determine exactly what your customers want to know about more often. That means higher conversions!

## Expert to Watch: *Brian Clark*[119]

Brian Clark is a man that needs no introduction. As a serial entrepreneur and writer, Brian was one of the first voices on the scene in the world of digital content. Brian built three successful companies using online marketing, until he made the permanent shift to an online business model, when he founded Copyblogger.

---

119 Brian Clark, http://www.copyblogger.com/author/brian/

Copyblogger is one of the Internet's most popular websites where people can learn about content creation, copywriting, and selling on the Internet. Through this blog, Brian helps his readership build their companies from the ground up.

Copyblogger has won several awards, including being named one of the world's most powerful blogs. Brian has gone on to become one of the most influential online marketers on the planet, winning awards from major publications. It is rare to find a bestselling book on online marketing today without finding his name somewhere in its pages.

He has appeared in Seth Godin's books, and books by Joe Pulizzi, Darren Rowse, John Jantsch, and Michael Hyatt — all key players in the digital marketing field. Since his rise to top influencer, Brian has established a few other online companies, all of which have become successful due to his incredible online marketing talent.

Brian's real value lies in his writing. With a fresh, simple style, Brian shows his readers what it means to create engaging, interesting, and entertaining content all year round. He regularly gives away eBooks and is involved in an online learning platform called Unemployable, through which he teaches freelancers and startups how to succeed online.

We strongly suggest that you subscribe to Copyblogger right away. This man will teach you what it takes to create exceptional content in a world brimming with ordinary, boring things. It may also be useful to sign up at Unemployable.com, where you can enjoy weekly audio lessons and connect with industry leaders. Also be sure to follow Brian on Twitter @brianclark.

# 16

# IN-HOUSE SEO VS SEO PROFESSIONALS

*"If you think it's expensive to hire a professional to do the job, wait until you hire an amateur."*

Red Adair, Oil Well Firefighter

What is the difference between hiring an in-house SEO professional, doing SEO yourself, or opting to hire an SEO company? With so many bad practices and traps in the industry today, you need to understand which option will most benefit your business.

We hope that, by now, we've made a solid case for the importance of SEO and building a search engine-friendly website. You need to realize that nothing about SEO is *hard*, but it consists of *so many* moving parts. When you have a properly optimized website and a consistent content-driven SEO strategy in play, you are virtually guaranteed to improve your rankings.

## Making the Right Choice: In-house or Pro?

This critical choice boils down to your company's needs. If you choose to focus on reputation management while creating, amplifying, and distributing content through your carefully prepared online distribution channels, you can become very successful online.

As an entrepreneur, your main challenge is time. There are few people who have the time to create content on a consistent basis while also keeping up with, and adjusting to, algorithm updates as they occur. With small business owners already spread thin, it's unlikely they will find the time to single-handedly power an in-house SEO program. While ongoing (non-technical) SEO tasks should be in every business owner's wheelhouse, some of the work related to SEO auditing and on-page SEO setup will more than likely require outside professional help.

In terms of ongoing SEO tasks, there is no set formula or rule as to how much content you need for a successful SEO program. Much depends on the level of competition and Internet savvy in your niche, and your geographic scope. Here is a partial list of the types of recurring tasks that *could* be part of an effective SEO-centric, small business inbound marketing plan:

✓ Blog posts: at least two per month, but ideally four to eight per month
   - *Minimum 500 words per post, ideally 1,000+ words, with occasional in-depth posts of 1,500-2,500 words or more*

✓ Structured data and schema implementation sitewide and for all new content

✓ Social media posts: 50-200 posts per month spread across all major social channels

- ✓ Authored guest blog posts for relevant third-party sites: occasional
- ✓ Posted guest contributor blog posts to your site: occasional
- ✓ Videos posted to YouTube and embedded on website where appropriate
- ✓ Ongoing reputation management
- ✓ Citation management at major directory and review sites
- ✓ SEO task management and monthly tracking/reporting
- ✓ eBooks: target one to two eBooks per year
- ✓ Podcasts
- ✓ Presentations for slide sharing
- ✓ Ongoing backlink analysis
- ✓ Ongoing competitive analysis
- ✓ Ongoing Google Analytics and Google Search Console monitoring analysis
- ✓ Email marketing
- ✓ AdWords PPC and social media advertising
- ✓ Press releases
- ✓ Monitoring of Google Algorithm updates and adjustment of on-page and off-page SEO strategy: as needed
- ✓ Site security, content management system updates, and plugin updates
- ✓ Marketing automation for lead capture and remarketing

In competitive niches, there is a very good chance that you will need to hire or delegate some of your SEO and *content marketing* tactics to an in-house team member or to a professional agency. By reading this book, you have gained a solid understanding of how important it is to transform your website into a *lead generating asset*.

Ignoring Google altogether is no longer an option. Instead, you need to sit down with the other people in your business and decide whether you're going to roll up your sleeves and do it yourself, hire a permanent staff member, or get some agency help.

The first thing you will need to do is outline your SEO budget and your website goals. These need to be aligned in order to work.

You cannot, for example, have almost no SEO budget but expect to be getting thousands of new organic visitors to your website within a few short months after launch. [120] We advise you to invite an SEO expert to weigh in on what is possible within your budget. Keep in mind that every dollar dedicated to implementing SEO best practices should, over time, put many more dollars back in your pocket. This is the ultimate function of a lead generation asset, especially your website.

Once you understand your budget and goals, the next step is to decide between a digital agency and a team member. For small businesses, an agency works well because it offers turn-key services — meaning, you don't have any training or managing responsibilities.

*Working with* a reputable SEO agency that uses best-practices SEO is ideal for most businesses. *Finding* an SEO agency that can deliver consistent results is another story. There are many great SEO consultants and agencies around the world. The problem is that for every good agency out there, there are 100 more selling shady SEO services. The onus is on you, the business owner or CEO, to do the due diligence required to find the right long-term SEO partner. As we suggested earlier, just treat SEO service procurement as you would filling a key employee position, and quality SEO companies will be easy to spot.

---

120 Andre Alpar, In-house SEO, SEO Agency or Both? 17 Points To Consider, http://searchenginewatch.com/sew/how-to/2173282/-house-seo-seo-agency-consider

## Why In-house is Always Hard!

Hiring in-house SEO personnel can also be a challenge, as many businesses have already discovered from past experience.

In very competitive niches, SEO experience makes a big difference. Yet, it can be a real challenge to find and hire a talented SEO person in-house, especially for small businesses with limited resources and budgets. The best search engine optimization specialists have their own agencies and are rarely available for full-time hire.

SEO is a talent-based profession. In some ways, it's similar to legal services. While you can have in-house legal staff for day-to-day legal issues, when push comes to shove, most companies rely on external, top-notch law firms to get them results. SEO is no different. The stakes are high and mistakes can be costly. Companies often get into trouble when they treat search engine optimization like a commodity service. You wouldn't price-shop for a surgeon, and you shouldn't price-shop for an SEO company to operate on your website.

This is why going with a proven agency is usually a better course of action. When you hire an agency, an SEO expert will outline his process and strategy. He will have experience working with other companies and dealing with ongoing SEO challenges in real time. As a matter of survival, SEO experts are forced to stay abreast of SEO and Google updates on a daily basis.

Hiring the wrong in-house SEO candidate, on the other hand, can be devastating. While he may produce some results, you will have to constantly check on what he is doing, and you may not know how to evaluate his effort or performance. You will never truly know if he is applying the latest SEO tactics. And he is only responsible to you, not to dozens of other demanding clients.

In 2016, the average annual salary for an entry-level SEO specialist in the US was over $40,000.[121] That means you are looking at spending

---

121 http://www.payscale.com/research/US/Job=Search_Engine_Optimization_(SEO)_Specialist/Salary/9804d65e/Entry-Level

around $3,500 a month just to hire an SEO specialist with minimal experience. For the same amount or less, you would be able to engage a highly experienced SEO agency, depending on the number and competition level of your keywords.

If you hire a full-time in-house SEO specialist, be sure to budget for ongoing training. To be effective, SEO specialists need to keep up with the latest trends and understand how and when to apply new tactics, adjust to new search engine updates, and stop using methods that fall out of favor.

It is also important to realize that agencies take a team-based approach and can help with things like content generation, which your in-house SEO staff may not be qualified to do. [122] If you choose to hire an SEO employee, you may need to outsource your ongoing content needs to a freelance writer. Digital agencies also have access to many premium SEO, social media, and tracking tools that you would otherwise have to pay for on your own.

Accountability is the real factor to consider when you make this decision, along with long-term impact. We absolutely believe that you will achieve greater success with a proven SEO agency than you would with an in-house SEO. That being said, there are many companies out there, especially larger ones, with world-class in-house SEO teams.

---

122 Jayson DeMers, Should You Manage SEO In-House or Work With an Agency, http://www.forbes.com/sites/jaysondemers/2015/04/29/should-you-manage-seo-in-house-or-work-with-an-agency/2/

## Common Questions in SEO: The Answers

There are many ways to screen an SEO agency before engaging one. Asking the right questions and demanding proof is the best way to make sure that you are not hiring a risky "fly-by night" service provider. Many SEO companies misrepresent their achievements and rarely even rank for their own services.

Unfortunately, the vast majority of people who hire SEO companies are disappointed in their results. This can be prevented by asking the right questions. Here are some of the most common SEO questions, along with the answers you should be looking for. [123]

 **QUICK TIP** Before you hire anyone, sit down with your SEO agency candidates and ask them hard questions. They should be able to answer them clearly and provide lots of proof to back up their claims. Because SEO is mostly data-based and tactical work, you should be shown a lot of numbers. Never hire a company that cannot prove its knowledge of SEO.

- **Have you done SEO for a business like mine before?** An SEO agency's sole purpose is to find you more customers. On the one hand, niche experience can be very helpful. On the other hand, if your SEO company is working for a direct competitor, that can be a pretty serious conflict of interest.

- **What references can you provide?** You are entitled to request a client list so that you can call these companies and get a first-

---

123 Josh Steimle, 10 Questions To Ask When Hiring An SEO Firm, http://www.entrepreneur.com/article/241485

hand account. Get the list and make the calls. Ask about attitudes, service, results, communication, reporting, and support. If an agency cannot give you at least five references, move on.

- **Can I see your recent case studies?** All top-notch SEO agencies create case studies to show their clients what they have done in the past. This is evidence of their successes with real people. You are entitled to ask if the clients were real, when the case studies were performed, and if the clients are still with the company.

- **What is the primary metric on which you focus your SEO?** This will throw off some companies, but it will help you eliminate pretenders from the pack. Real SEO experts focus on customer leads, sales, and conversions — not traffic and definitely not links. If they oversell traffic or link building, they might still be practicing old SEO.

- **What can you tell me about your approach to link building?** This question will reveal a lot about your SEO agency's beliefs and practices. You want to hear that the company values quality over quantity. A company that guarantees a set number of backlinks each month should be rejected. The best links are hard to get. As you know by now, they should mostly be talking about marketing strategy, content, and social media, as these are all key to SEO.

- **When will I begin to see results?** SEO is slow cooked, not microwaved. Expect legitimate companies to produce some initial results within 4-6 months, and better results within a year. SEO is a long-term commitment so any promotion of immediate results is suspicious.

- **What type of marketing or SEO-related certifications do you have?** The best SEO companies are led by seasoned pros with advanced degrees and industry certifications. Being AdWords-certified is a great sign, as are respected marketing certifications and designations. You will also find that, often, the best service providers are published authors, contributing authors on business websites, and frequent speakers at digital marketing events.

## How Much Does SEO Cost?

This is without a doubt the most common question asked in the SEO today. You will hear many different answers as you search for an SEO agency. We can tell you what to look out for when it comes to budgeting for SEO, so that your expectations are realistic.

With SEO, either you have a budget and a plan for success, or you don't. It's that simple. Without a properly funded plan, failure is inevitable. Compromise too much on your plan or budget, and you will fail.

As we have emphasized, SEO is not a short-term play. Keep in mind that long-term strategies require months and years get the best results, not days and weeks. With the constant changes to Google's algorithms, your SEO needs to be ongoing. You should expect some minimal results within the first year, but by the second year, you should be well on your way to crushing the competition.

"Cheap SEO" is a contradiction, and buying it will almost always get you into trouble. You cannot expect to pay $500 a month for cheap services and expect miracle results in return. Chances are you are doing more harm than good. Expect to spend a minimum of $1,000 per month for *basic* local SEO services. The sub-$1,000/month SEO fees is where most of the snake oil is sold. Most legitimate SEO companies will charge $2,000 to $5,000 per month, minimum. You should expect SEO agencies that service national and enterprise-class companies to *start* at $10,000 per month and higher.

*Forbes* has an excellent article on how to plan and budget for SEO, which was a major inspiration for this chapter. It may be one of the best articles written on the subject to date:

**http://www.forbes.com/sites/joshsteimle/2015/04/23/ how-to-plan-and-budget-for-seo/**

Before initiating any sort of contract with an SEO agency, meet the team in person. If the owner or representative of the SEO firm does not want to meet face-to-face, this is a big red flag. Many companies pretend to offer SEO services, then pass the work off to third parties. You never know where these people are or what they are doing. Meetings should precede engagement!

## Red Flags When Hiring an SEO Company

The last piece of advice you need is the ability to spot a fraudulent or unqualified company when you come across one. There are many bad SEO agencies out there. You may believe that you are getting a great deal, and you may even believe you have found a needle-in-the-haystack provider — but make sure to look out for the following red flags.

The location of your SEO firm is an issue. Of course, there are excellent SEO companies located all over the world. Unfortunately, many small businesses have run into trouble with offshore SEO service providers. And if a problem occurs, you have very little recourse. A reputable local (or at least domestic) company is less likely to disappear with your money, violate your contract, or risk using prohibited SEO techniques on your website.

Providers in other countries can sever ties, leaving you with a big mess. [124] You may find your website banned by Google with no support to fix it, because the offshore SEO company has suddenly vanished and will not return your calls. It's best to make sure that your SEO company is local and that they are transparent about who will be working on your account.

---

124 Phil Singleton, 12 Questions To Ask Before Hiring An SEO Firm, http://kcseopro.com/questions-to-ask-before-hiring-an-seo-firm/

Another red flag to look out for is being "handed off." The moment you have signed the contracts, you suddenly find yourself dealing with a new person — a junior in the company. The old bait and switch scam is as much a problem in SEO as it is in other service industries that have been around forever; do not fall for it or turn a blind eye if it happens to you.

As we have emphasized, SEO is a talent-based service, and you won't get the results you want if a trainee is suddenly managing your account. No one likes being fobbed off onto junior, less experienced staff members who are learning the business on your dime. It will slow down your progress and may even result in a botched campaign. You have to head this off at the pass.

The same can be said about outsourcing. It is a major red flag if your SEO firm is outsourcing *any* form of link building. SEO requires a variety of third-party tools and services to get the best results, but you are entitled to know which services are being used.

You should always be able to cancel your SEO service contract after some kind of initial term, perhaps after 3-6 months. Many SEO agencies will allow you to cancel anytime with 30 days written notice right from the start. Companies that want to lock you down with long-term contracts are just in it for the money. More importantly, there is less motivation to deliver good service every month when a long-term service contract is in place.

## Expert to Watch: *Josh Steimle*[125]

Josh Steimle has been a well-known thought leader in the SEO and digital marketing niche for years. As a speaker, writer, and businessman, few know as much about SEO as Josh.

Josh is the founder and CEO of MWI, a full-service digital marketing agency established in 1999. At MWI, Josh and his team focus on digital lead generation using a full suite of services including SEO, SEM,

---

125 About, http://www.joshsteimle.com/about/

social media marketing, content marketing, digital PR, conversion optimization, and email marketing. With offices in the US and Asia, MWI serves not just clients within Asian and Western markets, but has become the go-to company for businesses looking to expand from one market to the other.

Josh has written over 200 articles for publications like Forbes, Inc, Entrepreneur, Time, Mashable, and TechCrunch on the topics of SEO, social media, and content marketing. His recent book, *Chief Marketing Officers at Work* (Apress, 2016), gives a fly-on-the-wall perspective of what it's like to be a CMO or VP Marketing, and includes exclusive interviews with 29 CMOs and other top marketers from companies like GE, Spotify, Target, PayPal, and The Home Depot.

As a TEDx speaker, Josh has contributed to ever-evolving ideas about education and the Internet, reaching millions of people with his profound messages. He regularly presents at marketing and other business events worldwide speaking about how individuals and companies can use digital marketing to grow influence and revenue.

In 2001, while earning a Masters of Information Systems Management from Brigham Young University, Josh won his school's business plan competition for what has become MWI today. The next year, he and his partner were jointly named Young Entrepreneur of the Year by the Utah chapter of the Small Business Administration.

We highly recommend subscribing to Josh's posts on all of the major sites for which he writes and buying his book which is available for purchase on Amazon.

You can follow Josh through his website at JoshSteimle.com or on Twitter @joshsteimle.

# YOUR CALL TO ACTION

*"You and you alone determine whether or not you'll be successful in your business goals. There are no acceptable excuses in life. There's only action and inaction — and your choice of which road you decide to take."*

Rae Hoffman, PushFire

You have reached the end of this book and the beginning of your journey into modern search engine optimization. As a web designer, you should now see the value in adopting SEO best practices and embracing the principles of inbound marketing. The industry and your business simply will not survive without them.

As a business owner, entrepreneur, or marketer, you have learned that SEO is the way for your company to leverage Google in order to steal large chunks of market share from the competition. For small to medium-sized companies, an SEO-powered inbound marketing strategy is your ticket to rapid growth. To borrow from the *The Matrix* once again, this is your red pill/blue bill moment. Take a look at your current website with fresh eyes, and ask yourself if you are getting the most out of your online presence. It's time to stop getting your butt kicked online and start doing the kicking!

Imagine funnel-ready traffic coming in from your social media channels and even more pouring in from Google Search. With dedication and commitment, your website can become the lead generating asset you need it to be — fueling your company's growth for years to come.

Just like the advertising men of the sixties, you currently have a unique opportunity to become an early adopter and make strides with SEO before the copy-cats jump in. You can act right now and put some serious distance between your business and the competition.

Not only will you attract higher quality leads from prospects who are less price-sensitive, but you will also realize extended benefits by engaging with your online community. You will be able to streamline your business and improve products and services so your business can become the powerhouse you have always dreamed it could be.

Inbound marketing is here to stay. While all of your competitors scratch their heads and make half-assed attempts to succeed online, you can make it happen. Everything begins with your website, and you can't build a killer website without SEO! If your customers cannot find you, they cannot buy from you.

In closing, we'd like to share an inspirational analogy that AdWords expert Perry Marshall uses to explain his view of the corporate world and the two types of people that inhabit it.[126] You are either a wolverine or a poodle. Poodles get their food and water bowl filled every day, and yap for the things in life to which they feel entitled. They sleep on the couch and watch Seinfeld reruns with the kids. Their owners take them for trots down the sidewalk. Wolverines live in the woods, brave ice and snow, ferociously mark out large territories, sleep in the wild, and eat what they kill. Wolverines eat poodles.

---

126 Perry Marshall. Poodles vs. Wolverines. https://www.perrymarshall.com/29724/poodles-vs-wolverines/

With the principles, strategies, and tactics you have learned in this book, you are ready to be an ass-kicking SEO wolverine and make the coming year *your best year ever*.

To your success,

*-John Jantsch & Phil Singleton*

P.S. If you haven't done so already, please be sure to claim the bonus offers at:

**https://seoforgrowth.com/seo-book/**

P.S.S. Kindly leave a book review via this link:
http://www.seoforgrowth.reviews

# REFERENCES

## Chapter 1

*B2B Digital Evolution. Think With Google.* https://www.thinkwithgoogle.com/articles/b2b-digital-evolution.html

*When the Path to Purchase Becomes the Path to Purpose. Think With Google.* https://www.thinkwithgoogle.com/articles/the-path-to-purpose.html

http://www.michaelport.com

## Chapter 2

Nelson, Amanda, *30 Inspiring Marketing Quotes from SEO Experts,* http://www.exacttarget.com/blog/40-inspiring-marketing-quotes-from-seo-experts/

*Top 15 Most Popular Search Engines/August 2015,* http://www.ebizmba.com/articles/search-engines

*How Search Engines Operate,* https://moz.com/beginners-guide-to-seo/how-search-engines-operate

Hormby, Tom, *The Rise Of Google: Beating Yahoo at Its Own Game,* http://lowendmac.com/2013/the-rise-of-google-beating-yahoo-at-its-own-game/

*About Search Engine Land,* http://searchengineland.com/about

*About Marketing Land,* http://marketingland.com/about

Sullivan, Danny, *Google Now Handles At Least 2 Trillion Searches Per Year,* http://searchengineland.com/google-now-handles-2-999-trillion-searches-per-year-250247

Bullas, Jeff, *10 Facts Reveal The Importance of Ranking High In Google,* http://www.jeffbullas.com/2010/07/14/10-facts-reveal-the-importance-of-ranking-high-in-google/

Sheridan, Marcus, *The Future Of SEO And Google's Search Algorithm 2015 & Beyond,* http://www.thesaleslion.com/future-google-seo-2015/

Murphy, Lincoln, *Demand Generation vs. Demand Capture,* http://inbound.org/post/view/demand-generation-vs-demand-capture

## Chapter 3

Nelson, Amanda, *40 Inspiring Marketing Quotes From SEO Experts,* http://www.exacttarget.com/blog/40-inspiring-marketing-quotes-from-seo-experts/

Schwartz, Barry, *Is eBay A Big Loser In Google's Panda 5.0 Update? – Winners & Losers Data,* http://searchengineland.com/panda-4-0s-big-loser-ebay-winners-losers-chart-192123

*2011 Updates,* https://moz.com/google-algorithm-change#2011

*Difference Between Google Panda And Google Penguin,* http://seoupdates.info/difference-between-google-panda-and-google-penguin/

Shewan, Dan, *How Google Hummingbird Changed The Future Of Search,* http://www.wordstream.com/blog/ws/2014/06/23/google-hummingbird

Patel, Neil, *Everything You Need To Know About Google's Local Algorithm Pigeon,* http://searchengineland.com/everything-need-know-pigeon-algorithm-211771

Allen, Tim, *Life Above And Beyond The Fold,* https://moz.com/blog/life-above-and-beyond-the-fold

Schwartz, Barry, *Biography,* https://www.rustybrick.com/barry

Perez, Sarah, *Google's "Mobile Friendly" Update Could Impact Over 40% Of Fortune 500 Websites,* http://techcrunch.com/2015/04/21/googles-mobile-friendly-update-could-impact-over-40-of-fortune-500/#.fqnm6k:GqPe

Fishkin, Rand, *How To Handle A Google Penalty – And, An Example From The Field Of Real Estate,* https://moz.com/blog/how-to-handle-a-google-penalty-and-an-example-from-the-field-of-real-estate

## Chapter 4

Edgecomb, Carolyn, *24 Inbound Marketing Quotes To Inspire You,* http://www.impactbnd.com/blog/24-inbound-marketing-quotes-inspire-you

*The Inbound Methodology,* http://www.hubspot.com/inbound-marketing

*What is Content Marketing,* http://contentmarketinginstitute.com/what-is-content-marketing/

Steimle, Josh, *What Is Content Marketing?* http://www.forbes.com/sites/joshsteimle/2014/09/19/what-is-content-marketing/

Handley, Ann, *Press,* http://www.annhandley.com/press/

*What Is Content Authority?* https://www.marketingtechblog.com/what-is-content-authority/

Honigman, Brian, *How To Use Content Marketing To Build Authority And Subject Matter Expertise,* http://www.skyword.com/contentstandard/art-of-storytelling/how-to-use-content-marketing-to-build-authority-and-subject-matter-expertise/

*Developing A Content Marketing Strategy,* http://contentmarketinginstitute.com/developing-a-strategy/

Gudema, Louis, *How Guest Blogging Solved My SEO Problem,* http://contentmarketinginstitute.com/2015/02/guest-blogging-seo-problem/

Patel, Neil, *15 Types Of Content That Will Drive You More Traffic,* http://www.quicksprout.com/2014/04/14/how-these-15-types-of-content-will-drive-you-more-traffic/

## Chapter 5

Godin, Seth, *Pretty Websites,* http://sethgodin.typepad.com/seths_blog/2015/05/pretty-websites.html

Jones, William, *How To Get High Google Rankings For Your Website In 2015,* http://www.seoireland.net/how-to-get-high-google-rankings-for-your-website-in-2015/

Singleton, Phil, *Boosting Conversions: 11 Experts Share Their Secrets,* http://www.webdesignerdepot.com/2015/05/boosting-conversions-11-experts-share-their-secrets/

*7 Secrets Graphic Designers Won't Tel You About Effective Website Design,* https://blog.kissmetrics.com/graphic-designer-secrets/

Southern, Matt, *SEO And Content Marketing: How To Find The Perfect Balance Between Both,* http://positionly.com/blog/seo/seo-content-marketing

Harter, Justin, *21 Reasons Why You Shouldn't Use DIY Site Builders,* http://superpixel.co/21-reasons-shouldnt-use-site-builder/

Odden, Lee, *Where Social Media And SEO Fit In Today's Content Marketing Mix,* http://www.toprankblog.com/2015/06/integrated-social-seo-content/

Enge, Eric, *About,* https://www.stonetemple.com/about-eric-enge/

## Chapter 6

*50 Awesome Quotes To Guide Your Direct Traffic Digital Marketing Strategy,* http://www.profoundry.co/50-awesome-quotes-to-guide-your-digital-marketing-strategy/

*A Website Is Not Enough: How To Build An Online Marketing Strategy And Measure Results,* http://wordpress.tv/2013/12/04/a-web-site-is-not-enough-how-to-build-an-online-marketing-strategy-and-measure-results/

*The Difference Between Strategy And Tactics,* http://www.web-strategist.com/blog/2013/01/14/the-difference-between-strategy-and-tactics/

Shewan, Dan, *How To Create A Ferocious Unique Selling Proposition,* http://www.wordstream.com/blog/ws/2014/04/07/unique-selling-proposition

Vaughan, Pamela, *How To Create Detailed Buyer Personas For Your Business (Free Persona Template),* http://blog.hubspot.com/blog/tabid/6307/bid/33491/Everything-Marketers-Need-to-Research-Create-Detailed-Buyer-Personas-Template.aspx

Klausner, Andrew, *Creating A Successful Marketing Strategy,* http://www.forbes.com/sites/advisor/2013/04/17/creating-a-successful-marketing-strategy/

Aicardi, Sergio, *7 Key Pieces Of Advice About Web Content Strategy From Matt Cutts,* http://contentmarketinginstitute.com/2015/01/advice-web-content-strategy-matt-cutts/

*About Duct Tape Marketing,* http://www.ducttapemarketing.com/about

## Chapter 7

Fishkin, Rand, *100 SEO Tips And Tweetable Quotes From Rand Fishkin,* http://mysiteauditor.com/blog/rand-fishkin-quotes/

*SEO Glossary – The Searchmetrics Dictionary Of Search Engine Optimization, Page-Title,* http://www.searchmetrics.com/glossary/page-title/

*SEO Glossary – The Searchmetrics Dictionary Of Search Engine Optimization, Description,* http://www.searchmetrics.com/glossary/page-description/

*SEO Glossary – The Searchmetrics Dictionary Of Search Engine Optimization, Alt Attributes,* http://www.searchmetrics.com/glossary/alt-attributes/

Kapusta, Stephen, *Target Adwords Competitor Keywords The Right Way,* http://www.lunametrics.com/blog/2015/05/13/target-adwords-competitor-keywords-rlsa/

*Using Keyword Planner To Get Keyword Ideas And Traffic Forecasts,* https://support.google.com/adwords/answer/2999770?hl=en

*Google AdWords Keyword Tool Is A Beginner Keyword Research Tool,* http://www.wordstream.com/adwords-keyword-tool

*SEO Driven Approach To Content Marketing,* http://coschedule.com/blog/content-marketing-seo/

Reich, David, *Where And When Your Keywords Really Matter For Content Marketing And SEO,* http://contentmarketinginstitute.com/2011/10/keywords-for-content-marketing-and-seo/

Kim, Larry, *Founder And Chief Technology Officer,* http://www.wordstream.com/larry-kim

## Chapter 8

*Top 20 Inspirational SEO Quotes Of All-Time,* http://magnetsites.com/top-20-inspirational-seo-quotes-time/

Travers, Dorian, *Web Design vs. SEO Finding The Balance,* http://www.mycustomer.com/blogs-post/web-design-vs-seo-finding-balance/164971

Patel, Neil, *How To Perform An SEO Audit – Free $5000 Template Included,* http://www.quicksprout.com/2013/02/04/how-to-perform-a-seo-audit-free-5000-template-included/

Webb, Steve, *How To Perform The World's Greatest SEO Audit,* https://moz.com/blog/how-to-perform-the-worlds-greatest-seo-audit

*How To Boost Your SEO By Using Schema Markup,* https://blog.kissmetrics.com/get-started-using-schema/

Shepard, Cyrus, *Announcing The Web Developer's SEO Cheat Sheet,* https://moz.com/blog/seo-cheat-sheet

*Beginner's Guide To SEO, The Basics Of Search Engine Friendly Design & Development,* https://moz.com/beginners-guide-to-seo/basics-of-search-engine-friendly-design-and-development

Shepard, Cyrus, *More Than Keywords: 7 Concepts Of Advanced On-Page SEO,* https://moz.com/blog/7-advanced-seo-concepts?utm_content=buffer347a7&utm_medium=social&utm_source=linkedin.com&utm_campaign=buffer

Schwartz, Barry, *Google Updates Its Page Layout Algorithm To Go After Sites "Top Heavy" With Ads,* http://searchengineland.com/google-updates-page-layout-algorithm-go-sites-top-heavy-ads-183929

*Nine Best Practices For Optimized < Title > Tags,* http://searchengineland.com/nine-best-practices-for-optimized-title-tags-111979

*About Joost de Valk,* https://yoast.com/about-us/joost-de-valk/

## Chapter 9

Von, Fervil, *10 Best SEO Quotes From Top Internet Marketing Influencers,* http://www.fervilvon.com/10-best-seo-quotes-from-top-Internet-marketing-influencers/

Fox, Vanessa, *New York Times Exposes J.C. Penney Link Scheme That Causes Plummeting Rankings In Google,* http://searchengineland.com/new-york-times-exposes-j-c-penney-link-scheme-that-causes-plummeting-rankings-in-google-64529

Schwartz, Barry, *Google Webmaster Tools Rebrands To Google Search Console,* http://searchengineland.com/google-webmaster-tools-rebrands-to-google-search-console-221282

Haynes, Marie, *Your Start-To-Finish Guide To Using Google's Disavow Tool,* https://moz.com/blog/guide-to-googles-disavow-tool

Nelson, Anthony, D, *Broken Link Building Guide: From Noob to Novice,* https://moz.com/blog/broken-link-building-guide-from-noob-to-novice

Van Der Graaf, Peter, *Backlink Monitoring: Keeping Track of Your Existing Links,* http://searchenginewatch.com/sew/how-to/2271355/backlink-monitoring-keeping-track-of-your-existing-links

*About Neil Patel,* http://www.quicksprout.com/about/

## Chapter 10

Van Der Beld, Bas, *Remarkable Quotes From "SEO Now", Do You Agree?* http://www.stateofdigital.com/remarkable-quotes-seo-now/

Anderson, Myles, *88% Of Consumers Trust Online Reviews As Much As Personal Recommendations,* http://searchengineland.com/88-consumers-trust-online-reviews-much-personal-recommendations-195803

Aspland, George, *Local Businesses: How To Get Good Online Reviews That Build Business,* http://searchengineland.com/local-businesses-get-good-online-reviews-build-business-214939

Skipsey, Caroline, *Marketing: What's Your Strategy For Dealing With Online Reviews?* https://www.brandwatch.com/2015/05/the-power-of-online-reviews-whats-your-brand-strategy/

*Managing Your Online Reviews,* http://smallbiztrends.com/2014/09/managing-your-online-reviews.html

Dietrich, Gini, *Seven Tips To Building Your Brand's Reputation Online,* http://www.inc.com/theupsstore/seven-tips-to-building-your-brands-reputation-online.html

Bernstein, Brenda, *How To Maximize Your LinkedIn Endorsements,* http://www.socialmediaexaminer.com/manage-linkedin-endorsements/

## Chapter 11

*Social Media Quotes,* http://www.brainyquote.com/quotes/keywords/social_media.html

Rayson, Steve, *Content, Shares, and Links: Insights from Analyzing 1 Million Articles,* https://moz.com/blog/content-shares-and-links-insights-from-analyzing-1-million-articles

Enge, Eric, *Do Social Signals Drive SEO,* http://www.convinceandconvert. com/digital-marketing/do-social-signals-drive-seo/

*Help Customers Find You: How To Use Keywords On Your Social Networks,* https://blog.kissmetrics.com/help-customers-find-you/

Pascale, Angie, *7 Legitimate Ways That Social Media Impacts SEO,* http://www.clickz. com/clickz/column/2342211/7-legitimate-ways-that-social-media-impacts-seo

*Chris Brogan,* https://en.wikipedia.org/wiki/Chris_Brogan

## Chapter 12

*10 Great SEO Quotes,* http://www.clickfire.com/10-great-seo-quotes/

*Search Ranking Factors 2015,* http://www.searchmetrics.com/knowledge-base/ranking-factors/

Martin, James, A, *Top 10 Things To Look For In An SEO Expert,* http://www. cio.com/article/2400260/careers-staffing/top-10-things-to-look-for-in-an-seo-expert.html

Fishkin, Rand, *About,* https://moz.com/about/team/randfish

## Chapter 13

Ries, Eric, *Quotes,* http://www.brainyquote.com/quotes/quotes/e/ericries512162.html

*Google Adwords, Benefits,* https://www.google.com/adwords/benefits/

Kim, Larry, *The War On 'Free' Clicks: Think Nobody Clicks On Google Ads? Think Again!* http://www.wordstream.com/blog/ws/2012/07/17/google-advertising

*How To Know What Root Keywords Rank Well In Search Engines,* http://wpcurve.com/root-keywords/

Eppinger, Nick, *Essential Guide To Testing Adwords Ad Copy – Part 1,* http://www.lunametrics.com/blog/2015/08/03/adwords-testing-guide-part-1/

*Adwords Trademark Policy,* https://support.google.com/adwordspolicy/answer/6118?hl=en

*Ready To Get Started?* https://www.google.com/adwords/get-started/

*Using Keyword Matching Options,* https://support.google.com/adwords/answer/2497836?hl=en

## Chapter 14

Dykes, Brent, *31 Essential Quotes On Analytics And Data,* http://www.analyticshero.com/2012/10/25/31-essential-quotes-on-analytics-and-data/

Coren, Yehoshua, *The Importance Of Clean And Meaningful Google Analytics,* http://www.analytics-ninja.com/blog/2013/02/getting-clean-and-meaningful-google-analytics-data.html

*How To Do A/B Split Testing In WordPress Using Google Analytics,* http://www.wpbeginner.com/wp-tutorials/how-to-ab-split-testing-in-wordpress-using-google-analytics/

*The Business Benefits Of Google Analytics,* http://www.koozai.com/blog/analytics/google-analytics-business-benefits/

*Analytics,* http://www.google.com/analytics/learn/index.html

*Making Search More Secure,* http://googleblog.blogspot.com/2011/10/making-search-more-secure.html

*Analytics Help,* https://support.google.com/analytics/answer/1009409?hl=en

*What Is Search Console?* https://support.google.com/webmasters/answer/4559176?hl=en

Schwartz, Barry, *Google Webmaster Tools Adds Blocked Resources Report & Updates Fetch & Render Tool,* http://searchengineland.com/google-webmaster-tools-adds-blocked-resources-report-updates-fetch-render-tool-216558

*Site Map,* http://www.techopedia.com/definition/5393/site-map

*About Glenn Gabe, http://www.gsqi.com/about-glenn-gabe/*

## Chapter 15

Yan, Carrie, *Top 10 SEO Quotes: A Visual Representation,* http://www.poweredbysearch.com/top-10-seo-quotes/

Vertommen, Kevin, *Everything You Need to Know About Google Search Console,* http://webdesign.tutsplus.com/articles/everything-you-need-to-know-about-google-search-console--cms-24069

Hussain, Anum, *15 Insider Tips For Creating A Content Creation Machine*

*(Slideshare)*, http://blog.hubspot.com/marketing/tips-to-build-a-marketing-content-machine

*Your Guide To Content Curation For SEO,* http://www.searchenginejournal.com/guide-content-curation-seo/80773/

Patel, Sujan, *37+ Tips And Resources For Building A Fine-Tuned Content Marketing Machine From The Ground Up,* https://blog.bufferapp.com/37-tips-resources-building-fine-tuned-content-marketing-machine-ground

Murray, Mike, *4 Online Content Best Practices For Success,* http://contentmarketinginstitute.com/2014/01/online-content-best-practices-for-2014/

Clark, Brian, *Webinar: Smart Systems And Processes For Freelancers, Solopreneurs, And Startups,* http://www.copyblogger.com/author/brian/

## Chapter 16

Nelson, Amanda, *40 Inspiring Marketing Quotes From SEO Experts,* http://www.exacttarget.com/blog/40-inspiring-marketing-quotes-from-seo-experts/

Alpar, Andre, *In-House SEO, SEO Agency, Or Both? 17 Points To Consider,* http://searchenginewatch.com/sew/how-to/2173282/-house-seo-seo-agency-consider

*SEO Entry-Level Salary,* http://www.payscale.com/research/US/Job=Search_Engine_Optimization_(SEO)_Specialist/Salary/9804d65e/Entry-Level

De Mers, Jayson, *Should You Manage SEO In-House Or Work With An Agency?* http://www.forbes.com/sites/jaysondemers/2015/04/29/should-you-manage-seo-in-house-or-work-with-an-agency/2/

*10 Questions To Ask When Hiring An SEO Firm,* http://www.entrepreneur.com/article/241485

Steimle, Josh, *How To Plan And Budget For SEO,* http://www.forbes.com/sites/joshsteimle/2015/04/23/how-to-plan-and-budget-for-seo/

*12 Questions To Ask Before Hiring An SEO Firm,* http://kcseopro.com/questions-to-ask-before-hiring-an-seo-firm/

*About,* http://www.joshsteimle.com/about/

# ABOUT THE AUTHORS

## JOHN JANTSCH

John Jantsch has been called the World's Most Practical Small Business Expert for consistently delivering proven real-world, small business marketing ideas and strategies.

He is the creator of the Duct Tape Marketing System and Duct Tape Marketing Consulting Network which trains and licenses small business marketing consultants around the world.

John frequently consults with small and mid-sized businesses, helping them create marketing plans and organized marketing systems that smooth the way for steady growth.

He is a veteran speaker and workshop leader with over 500 successful events under his belt.

His blog was chosen as a *Forbes* favorite for marketing and small business and his podcast, The Duct Tape Marketing Podcast — a top-ten marketing show on iTunes — was called a "must listen" by *Fast Company* magazine.

*Huffington Post* calls John one of the top 100 "Must Follow" on Twitter, and *Forbes* named Duct Tape Marketing (www.ducttapemarketing.com) one of the 100 Best Websites for Entrepreneurs.

He is the featured marketing contributor to American Express OPENForum and is a popular workshop and webinar presenter for organizations such as American Express, Intuit, Verizon, HP, and Citrix.

John's practical take on small business is often cited as a resource in publications such as the *Wall Street Journal, New York Times,* and CNNMoney.

As Seth Godin puts it, "John Jantsch is the Peter Drucker of small business marketing tactics."

## Phil Singleton

Phil Singleton is a self-described "SEO grunt" obsessed with tweaking websites for search engine optimization and functional performance. He is a Duct Tape Marketing Certified Consultant and holds a B.S. in Finance from Fairfield University, as well as an MBA from Thunderbird, The Graduate School of International Management in Phoenix, Arizona.

Phil is a co-author of the Award-winning, Amazon best-seller **The Small Business Owner's Guide To Local Lead Generation and author of the Amazon best-seller *How To Hire A Web Designer: And Not Get Burned By Another Agency.***

In addition to providing inbound marketing consulting services to companies across the United States Phil provides custom SEO-friendly websites under the brand Kansas City Web Design® at KCWebDesigner. Com and online marketing and search engine optimization services under the brand Kansas City SEO® at KCSeoPro.com.

Phil is an active blogger, and his content has been featured at Duct Tape Marketing, Freshbooks, SEMRush.com, Ahrefs.com,

AdvancedWebRanking.com, WebDesignerDepot.com, and many local Kansas City and Midwest regional print publications and media sites.

Over the course of his career, Phil has helped dozens of US start-ups and tech companies raise millions of dollars in strategic venture capital investment and cross-border licensing agreements in the Asia Pacific region; run the global retail and online sales divisions for a best-selling line of consumer software products; and started a software company in Asia, raising venture capital funding, growing it to profitability with 25 employees, and then selling it three years later. The latter experience is what got him into SEO and Internet marketing — in short, by following the ROI trail to SEO.

Phil is fluent in Mandarin Chinese and has lived and traveled extensively in Asia for over ten years, based in Taipei, Taiwan, with stints in Beijing, Shanghai, and Hong Kong. He currently lives in Overland Park, Kansas with his wife Vivian and twin sons, Ely and Ostyn.

Printed in Great Britain
by Amazon